Fabulous
Framing

Milner Craft Series
Fabulous FRAMING

JOYCE SPENCER

Please use the designs and finishes for personal and private projects, teaching and profit. These finishes can be used by painters in competitions and exhibitions. Copyright does not extend to commercial use. However, the author would be grateful that acknowledgments and credit be given for original idea and inspiration, when teaching.

Joyce Spencer

First published in 2000 by
Sally Milner Publishing Pty Ltd
PO Box 2104
Bowral NSW 2576
AUSTRALIA

© Joyce Spencer 2000

Design by Ken Gilroy
Photography by Sergio Santos
Editing by Lyneve Rappell

Printed in Hong Kong

National Library of Australia Cataloguing-in-Publication data:

Spencer, Joyce.
Fabulous Framing.

ISBN 1 86351 248 9

1. Picture frames and framing.
2. Decoration and ornament.
I. Title. (Series: Milner craft series).

749.7

Disclaimer
The information in this instruction book is presented in good faith. However, no warranty is given, nor results guaranteed, nor is freedom from any patent to be inferred. Since we have no control over the information contained in this book, the publisher and the author disclaim liability for untoward results.

FOREWORD

The French painter Nicholas Poussin commented that a picture needs a frame in order that the eye shall remain concentrated, and not dispersed beyond the limits of the picture. A frame draws the eye to the image it surrounds. A well chosen frame enhances a picture.

Since the Middle Ages, artists have experimented with different methods of framing their work. Some of the earliest frames were not real frames at all but painted gold or floral borders in medieval prayer books and other manuscripts. During the Renaissance, when painters adopted canvas as their surface of choice, they added elaborate carved and gilded frames of plaster and wood. The tradition of complementing paintings with attractive frames continues to this day.

Certainly a beautiful painting deserves an appropriate frame. But so do many other images: a family photo, a special postcard, a child's painting, a collage, a sketch and so on.

Over the years Joyce Spencer has decorated a number of frames. You'll find several in her last book *Folk Art Wedding*. A couple of years ago Joyce decided that painted frames really warranted a book to themselves and *Fabulous Framing* is the result.

In this exciting collection Joyce combines her special interests, folk art and faux finishes. The book, however, goes far beyond the subject of frames. Joyce shares with you a wealth of product information and many tips for successful painting.

If you are a novice to the field of brushstrokes and paint effects, you will find the instructions comprehensive and easy to follow. The experienced painter will also draw inspiration from within these pages. There are new perspectives on familiar techniques such as marbling. You'll also discover some fun ideas like faux leather, denim and patchwork as well as texture and relief effects. And you don't need to confine these techniques to frames – they could be used on a range of surfaces. As an added bonus, most of the materials are inexpensive.

Joyce's enthusiasm for her subject is contagious. Browse through the pages. I am sure *Fabulous Framing* will soon have you in a creative frame of mind.

Deborah Kneen 1999

6

CONTENTS

Acknowledgments	9
Introduction	11
GETTING STARTED	12
Requirements	13
Paints	13
Brushes	13
Specialty paints	14
Mediums	14
General equipment	15
Preparation	15
Sanding	15
Sealing	16
Basecoating	16
Strokes & brush techniques	16
Round brush comma strokes	17
Double loading	18
Liner brush work	18
Flat brush blending	18
The dagger brush	19
Dots	20

Techniques & finishes	20
Fantasy tortoiseshell	20
Sponging	21
Leather look	22
Verdigris	22
Dry brushing	23
Denim	23
Patchwork	23
Texturing	23
Crackling	24
Distressing timber	24
Lapis lazuli	25
Marbling	25
Tortoiseshell	25
Fantasy marbling	26
Distressing paint	26
Slip slap	27
Gold leafing or gilding	27
Gold work	27
Dragging	28
Washes	28
Spattering	29
Antiquing	29
Tracing	30
Varnishing	32

THE PROJECTS   33

Frames   **Techniques & finishes**

Fantasy tortoiseshell frame   33   Fantasy tortoiseshell
Seaside frame   35   Sponging, texturing, dry brushing, varnishing
Blue dolphin frame   39   Distressed paint
Leather frame   41   Leather look, distressed paint
Olde leather frame   42   Leather look, distressed paint, antiquing
Musical angels frame   43   Verdigris, dry brushing, slip slap
Baby boy frame   47   Dry brushing
Line dancing frame   49   Denim, dry brushing, liner brush work
Patchwork frame   51   Patchwork, dots, comma strokes, varnishing
Flotsam & jetsam   55   Texturing, dry brushing, crackling
Olde crackled frame   57   Crackling, washes, dry brushes
Distressed daisy frame   61   Distressed timber, texturing, dry brushing, slip slap
Wedding frame   63   Gold work, sponging, dry brushing
Gold cherub frame   67   Gold work, dry brushing, texturing
Lapis lazuli frame   69   Lapis lazuli, spattering, sponging, liner brush work
Green marble frame   73   Fantasy marbling, sponging, spattering, varnishing
Small tortoiseshell frame   76   Tortoiseshell, washes, dragging, varnishing
Medium tortoiseshell frame   78   Tortoiseshell, washes, dragging, varnishing
Large tortoiseshell frame   78   Tortoiseshell, washes, dragging, varnishing
Baby girl's frame   83   Fantasy marbling, flat brush blending, liner work
Cute teddy frame   87   Distressed paint, dagger brush, tracing
Red & gold frame   89   Slip slap, dry brushing
Gold leafed mirror   92   Gold leafing, spattering, antiquing

I would like to sincerely thank the new owners and publishers of Sally Milner Publishing, Libby Renney and Ian Webster for their enthusiasm and professionalism. It has been a pleasure to meet and work with them. I wish them every success.

I would also like to thank Lyneve for her editing skills, and Ken and Sergio for their professionalism and stunning graphics.

To Deborah Kneen, my many thanks for writing the Foreword and for being my friend. Since we co-authored The Art of Teaching Craft, our paths have meandered in different directions but meeting up again in other places and activities, but always with affection, respect and joy in painting.

Joyce Spencer

I have loved messing around with paints since learning to paint in the folk and decorative style, having lessons, attending workshops, painting with friends and having time to experiment with the many mediums, specialty paints, and painting on different surfaces such as old suitcases, paper, metal, ceramic and wood.

In this book, picture, photo and mirror frames are used to show *faux* (or fake), fantasy or surface effects to paint, to set off a favourite painting scene or photo or interesting items such as embroidery.

I have great fun hunting for frames. They are found in chemists, discount, craft and art shops, supermarkets and even the odd garage sale. Existing frames in your home could perhaps do with a 'frame lift'. Your personal painted touch on a frame makes a lovely gift. You will be in great demand and become famous for them.

Often we are asked to donate something painted for raffles, fetes and fund raising. You could also create something special for commemorative events like weddings, anniversaries, christenings and Christmas. Hand painted frames are very saleable.

Many items can be framed: baby's first curls, old lace, old cards, a favourite poem, household sayings, pressed flowers, painted items on craft wood or paper, an old sampler or embroidery for example. A child's first drawing or painting is worthy of a frame.

Painting offers endless possibilities. The finishes used on the frames are but an introduction to painting on larger items such as furniture and trunks.

People have been decorating their homes since the earliest times, from cave painting with different hands, shapes and clay, to tombs and castles. The ancient Egyptians in particular had mastered the art of *faux* finishes. Only the wealthy could afford the real thing like marble columns, lapis lazuli, jewels, gold and silver. This gave artists the opportunity to copy early surviving decorative techniques.

Today, with modern tools, research, paints and media, we can copy some of these techniques in a matter of minutes. Fantasy marbling for instance can be done with plastic wrap. Distemper and plaster are replaced by quick drying acrylic gesso and paste.

The products used in this book are water based and nontoxic, which makes for a quick clean up.

Just as we all see colour differently, so is our approach to painting. Some of us have a lighter touch, others a heavier hand and a more robust approach. This factor is not important. It is the final result and the wonderful expressive feeling of accomplishment we receive when painting frames.

I started painting at a later stage in my life, and this has brought me great joy and many friends. I feel the need to paint or prepare something each day. Painting is good for my soul.

I hope you will find these frames, fun, rewarding, pleasurable and profitable to paint.

INTRODUCTION

The best way to
start painting
frames is to read
the book through,
choose a frame to
paint, and read
the step-by-step
instructions for
that project.

GETTING STARTED

Buy only the paints, brushes, mediums, etc., for the frame you first choose to do. This begins your basic stock and can be added to as needed. Make a shopping list for these requirements.

Some items, such as plastic wrap, pens, saucers or lids for paint, pencils, tracing paper, paper towels, cotton buds, jars and old toothbrushes, can be found around the house.

Paints are found in art, craft and folk art shops. Buy the best brushes you can afford. Some shops offer a mail order service.

If you are fortunate in having a spare spot to paint, great! Then you do not have to pack everything away. Wherever you work, it is best to protect the area by putting down some newspaper or old towels. Keep your brushes upright in a jar. Store the paints and mediums out of the reach of little children. The products used are mostly nontoxic but it is always better to play safe. Read all the labels carefully.

Requirements

Paints

Most of the paints, mediums and varnishes recommended in this book are Jo Sonja products, manufactured by Chroma Australia Pty Ltd. They are specially formulated for our frames. When a specific paint is needed the brand name is given. The paint comes in tubes or bottles and will last a long time if it is looked after properly.

Using one brand means that the products are compatible. Paints can be broken down with water and mediums. The consistency of the paint is important. A creamy mix is needed, a small amount of paint can be mixed with a small brush, but larger amounts should be mixed with a palette knife.

Please read all techniques carefully. Some paints and textures – like Deco Art's 'Sandstone' – contain glue, which means that some bottles have nozzles and applicators and others will need cheaper brushes.

Basecoat paints are usually available in a larger quantity and are more economical if painting several items the same colour. For one frame, tube paint mixed with a little sealer is an ideal basecoat. Please note that basecoat paints do not have the colour range that tube paints have.

Brushes

Good quality brushes are essential for stroke and refined painting. The bristles are synthetic and the type needed is listed with each project. Folk art brushes have short handles, the metal ferrules are round or flat and the size is imprinted on the handle. Each brush has a specific use. The dagger brush is a favourite of mine. The ferrule is flat but the bristles are cut at an acute angle so they have to be cleaned well. Chinese brushes are quite cheap and can be purchased at newsagencies. Foam brushes can also be used.

When painting, brushes need to be cleaned frequently to remove paint or when changing from one colour to another. Of course, they must also be cleaned at the end of each day's painting.

Painting-water should also be changed frequently and so should cleaning-water. When cleaning brushes, a cake of soap is needed. The wet brush should be worked back and forth on the soap and swished through water until it is clean. Repeat the process if the water shows colour or if you can see paint in the brush. Pat the brush dry on a paper towel. The addition of a little Jo Sonja's Retarder & Antiquing Medium into the brushes keeps them soft.

When using glue-based paints, such as some of the dimensional paints, the brushes need to be well cleaned. Some of these paints do have a nozzle or applicator and therefore no cleaning is needed.

Brushes may be kept flat or stood, bristles upright, in a jar. Never leave paint in your brush overnight.

Specialty paints

Dimensional paint is usually a glue-based product that dries hard in a mound, makes lines or dots. It is usually applied through a nozzle. Not all glue-based paints are dimensional. Sparkles and glitter will remain after the glue has dried flat and clear. Some metallic paints are dimensional – like fabric paints – but paints like the gold in tubes are not. Iridescent paints are similar. They can be diluted with water and used as washes over paint or used straight from the tube. Golds, for instance, are sometimes applied over a basecoat of red or yellow. The gold is supposed to glow.

Other dimensional acrylics are Textured Paste and Sandstones. While they have different drying times they are useful for fun effects and for filling holes.

As you can tell from these products, we have a large variety to choose from and there are always new products coming into the market to tempt us and to create new surface interests.

Mediums

These are specially formulated products. When mixed with paint or applied on top of paint they are most useful. For instance, when we add Jo Sonja's Retarder & Antiquing Medium to our paint it will slow down the drying time of the paint. The addition of Jo Sonja's Flow Medium will make the paint flow better for the fine detail work – like lace – without altering the colour. These products last for ages, as only a few drops are needed.

Another interesting product is Jo Sonja's Tannin Sealer &

Gold Size, which not only seals knots in wood to stop the sap from bleeding through the paint but it also doubles as a size for gold leafing.

Jo Sonja's Crackle Medium is another fun product to use. It makes cracks appear on the painted surface giving an aging effect.

Another product, which is purchased under the name of Rubbing Alcohol, or Isopropyl, is used in our work to soften paint. I call this technique 'leather look'.

General equipment
An old toothbrush
Cake of soap
Carbon pencil
Cotton balls
Cotton buds
Cotton gloves
Fine point stylus
Fine black pen
Graphite paper
Greaseproof paper
Gold leaf (dutch metal)
Hair dryer
Jar
Lint free rag
Magic tape
Notebook
Palette knife
Paper towels
Pencil
Plastic wrap
Plastic lids and bowls
Practice paper
Ruler
Scissors
Small feather
Sponges as listed
Water
Wet and dry sandpaper – fine, medium
Sandpaper – fine, medium & course

Preparation

Good preparation and groundwork are essential for a good result. Work in a well-lit area and keep your painting area clean. Choose only good quality frames and examine them carefully before you purchase them.

Sanding

Examine the frame. Fill any cracks with wood filler, acrylic paste or a quick-drying filler. Allow the filler to dry, and then sand the frame. Start with a coarse sandpaper to remove old varnish then use a fine one. Wipe or brush the dust away, do not blow. One way of testing for smoothness is to run your hand over the surface.

I like aluminium sandpaper on the timber. For a very fine

finish, I prefer a fine wet and dry paper even adding a little water to the surface. The layers of white on the 'Baby girl's frame' were done this way.

Sealing

It is always wise to seal our frames after sanding. Jo Sonja's All Purpose Sealer gives a 'tooth' for our paints to hold. The sealer can be applied with a chinese brush or added to the basecoat colour. Tilt the frame into the light to spot any ridges that may show through to the final coat of varnish. A very light sanding may be needed.

Basecoating

Put out enough paint to cover the frame. The paint needs to be a nice creamy consistency. Apply one coat with a foam or chinese brush. Allow the basecoat to dry and give the frame another coat if it is required in the instructions. Add sealer if necessary. Again tilt the frame to check for ridges or missed spots and, if needed, apply another coat. A light sanding with fine paper may be needed.

A hair dryer can be useful here. It is advisable to use a low heat setting. If it is too hot, the top layer dries leaving the underneath paint not quite dry.

Suitable brushes are the chinese or foam.

Stroke & brush techniques

The brush and stroke techniques used in this book require some practice. If you read the instructions, follow the step-by-step guide and practise, it will make learning easier.

Folk painting in the traditional way requires mastery of certain strokes relating to a particular style from a particular country, mostly European.

Each country had its own style of painting. From Bavaria the style called *bauermaleri*, from Holland came *hinderloopin*, and from Norway came *rosemaling*. One could spend a lifetime painting and studying one of these styles alone.

When we become addicted to folk painting, we want to learn everything at once. This book endeavours to cover just a few techniques which form the basis of the contemporary style of painting on frames.

Round brush comma strokes

Stroke work needs a combination of factors; the right brush for the stroke, a creamy consistency of paint, the correct pressure on the bristles and plenty of practice.

Folk art brushes have shorter handles and – when stroke making – they are held like a pencil. It is quite okay to rest your hand on your arm and roll the brush from side to side or to pull it up and down. Strokes can go in all directions and the frame can also be turned around. It is mostly when we paint large pieces of furniture, walls or ceilings that the strokes need to be painted in all directions. In many countries there were travelling painters whose work on homes survives today.

For large brush strokes and large areas of painting surface we need larger brushes. For small strokes and detailed work we need smaller brushes.

The chinese brushes, which are cheaper, are normally not used for stroke work.

To paint strokes with the round brush you will need:
- a palette
- water jar
- practice paper
- paper towel
- a tube of Jo Sonja's Acrylic Gouache, a darker colour
- No. 3 or 4 round brush

Squeeze a small amount of paint onto the palette. Mix to a creamy consistency with the water. When picking up the paint onto the brush, it is called 'loading' the brush and only practice will show you how much paint to pick up. Tap any excess onto a paper towel or onto the palette. Load your brush then, holding your brush like a pencil, place the bristles down on the practice paper with a little pressure. It should be a blob. Pick up a little more paint and this time apply more pressure to the bristles. Note how the bristles splay out. This time do not apply any pressure and pull down a fine line. Pick up more paint in your brush and make a blob. At the same time pull down a stroke releasing pressure on the bristles and lift off. You have made a stroke called a comma. It should resemble a daisy petal. Next, practise, practise, practise!

Another useful stroke is called the 'S'. It is good for painting borders, strokes and ribbons. The stroke is started with a line and no pressure, then pressure making a curve and then a fine line again with no pressure. While not quite a true 's', it is the straight line through it that makes this stroke.

Double loading

Double loading, or tipping, means that two colours of paint are put onto the brush for each stroke. This will give a highlight and make the stroke more interesting.

For instance, load the brush with a darker colour and pick up a lighter colour like gold, white or yellow on the tip of the brush and pull down. You will see a contrasting colour at the top coming down the stroke making a stripe.

Liner brush work

This is a small round brush with varying lengths of bristles. An 0 or 00 is usual. This brush is used for stroke work and making fine lines and outlines. The paint needs to be thinner than usual. Jo Sonja's Flow Medium is useful when mixed with paint and thinned for liner work. The colour does not change and the paint 'flows'. The brush is held upright and movement is from the shoulder so allow plenty of room.

The brush and paint need to flow, so that you can write, make ribbons and bows. Apply pressure for a thicker line. Please refer to the 'Cute teddy frame' for an example of this stroke.

Flat brush blending

The metal ferrule of these brushes is flattened so the size of the brush refers to the width. Some measurements may be in inches and others are numbered. A $1/4$" brush is used for the butterfly roses on the 'Baby girl's frame' and the 'Cute teddy frame'.

When first learning to paint everyone wants to paint roses. These are the hardest flowers to learn to paint, so this method was devised to help beginners. A different colour is picked up on each corner of the brush – usually a light and a dark – then worked into the brush making a third value in the middle. When making petals or shapes there is a light colour on top, shading down to the darker colour at the bottom. This stroke is made in all directions, from full strokes to half strokes.

To blend, you will need;
- practice paper
- red and white paint
- $1/4$" flat brush,

- blending paper such as greaseproof paper
- towel
- water

Put the two paints on the palette about 3 cm (1 $\frac{1}{4}$") long, like toothpaste on a brush.

Dip the bristles of the brush into the water. Tap some of the water onto a folded paper towel.

Pick up some red paint on one corner of the brush. Flip the brush over and pick up some white paint on the other corner. Blend back and forth on blending paper. The blending strip should be about an inch long and always move up towards the white.

At first you will have a red and white strip but gradually you will notice a pink value in the middle. You will need to examine the brush, pick up more paint and blend again before making another stroke. It is slow, but with practice you will understand blending. If the paint begins to merge into one colour, you will need to wash the brush and start again on a fresh blending strip.

On the practice paper, make a small crescent stroke. Hold the brush upright on the straight or chisel edge, go up a little and make an arch and come down. In other words; up, over and down. The white paint is on the top. This time, practise the reverse; down, over and up. This makes a bud or a bowl of the rose. The white stays at the top. Practise lots of these.

For the smaller base petals, blend more paint, turn your work around and make some short choppy strokes around this bowl. Keep the white to the outside. This stroke is tucked under to resemble petals on the rose, one or two strokes on each side and one across the bottom. Please refer to the colour work sheet for these roses and to the 'Cute teddy frame'.

If you feel the paint dragging, then start again. You may need a little more water in the brush. Jo Sonja's Stroke & Blending Medium can be worked into the brush but it is better to start with the basics and understand the process. If you are not happy with the result, the strokes can be repainted. The paint on your palette can be covered with plastic wrap so it does not dry out. Make a cup of coffee and repeat the process.

The dagger brush

This acutely angled brush has many uses. It makes leaves and ribbons. The colours on the brush can be more than one, and the paint can be opaque or thinned for background or watery leaves. The brush needs to be cleaned frequently. I keep all my brushes. The old ones make lovely ferns! Please refer to the 'Baby girl's frame' and the 'Cute teddy frame' where you will see groups of three leaves painted.

Set out your painting equipment. Pick up a little paint mixed with water. Tap off the excess on a paper towel. The size of the dagger brush for these leaves is a $1/4$" and is a flat brush.

Place the brush down lightly on the paper and it is a tiny fern leaf. Place the brush down on the paper again and pull over to the left and lift off. You have a leaf. Pick up more paint if necessary and pull a leaf over to the right and then one to the left. You now have a group of three leaves, which will be similar to rose leaves. Stems and veins can be painted with a fine liner brush.

Dots

Dots of varying sizes are made by picking up enough paint for each dot made with a stylus that has two different sized points. The end of a paintbrush is good for large dots, so is a satay stick or toothpick.

The dots can be made into little flowers. Small comma strokes can be pulled from the centre. Dots graduated in size make lovely borders. Please refer to the colour plate and the 'Patchwork frame'.

Techniques & finishes

There are many techniques used in painting frames. Some are modern and some have been borrowed from the past. Whatever the source, they are a lot of fun to do.

Modern mediums and paints add a sparkle and a new dimension to our frames. Please read all labels carefully, and note that climate conditions may affect some techniques such as crackling and varnishing.

Fantasy tortoiseshell

Fantasy tortoiseshell is a quick and easy way to achieve a very interesting finish. It is fun to do and requires only three tubes of paint. Other colour combinations are possible, so please experiment.

You will need:
- a palette
- one tube each of: Napthol Crimson, Burgundy, Rich Gold and Pale Gold
- Jo Sonja's 'Faux Finish' Kleister Medium
- a satay stick
- an index finger

Prepare the frame. Basecoat the frame with Burgundy. Depending on the size of the frame, put out a small amount of paint and an equal amount of the medium. Mix with the satay stick. Have some paper towels ready to wipe your finger.

Pick up a little Napthol Crimson on your index finger and lightly dab it on the frame. Pick up a little Pale and Rich Gold and dab it near the Crimson, then a dab of Burgundy, then Gold and Crimson. Go round the frame in this way.

The Kleister Medium will make little mounds of paint, and you will see the fingerprints in the paint. This is what we want to see. When the medium and paint dries, it will dry flat and leave this interesting finger finish. Small decorative buttons can be used to create designs too.

Apply two coats of satin or gloss varnish. Please refer to the colour plate for the 'Fantasy tortoiseshell frame'.

Sponging

Sponges, whether natural or synthetic, are another way of applying paint to a surface. When we refer to sponging, it is usually a way to blend several colours together quickly. Cover a small area with small sponges or a large area with larger sponges.

There are many types of sponges: sea, wool, synthetic; ones for cars, kitchens and laundries. Whatever the source, texture is what we look for. Please refer to the 'Seaside frame'.

To sponge you will need the following;
- paper towel
- a large bowl or ice cream container of water
- a ceramic sponge
- a disposable glove
- a palette containing several colours of paint
- practice paper or the back of the frame

Basecoat the frame if instructed in the project. Tightly wring out the sponge in water.

Pick up one colour – just a little – and dab it down lightly on the surface. If you press too hard there will be a blob. The idea is to press lightly, allowing the texture of the sponge to make the design. Apply in 'drifts' of colour.

Pick up another colour on another part of the sponge and repeat the dabbing. Pick up more paint and dab this colour near the first, where you will notice a change of colour. Dab lightly and quickly, blending colours and texture as you go. Turn the frame and sponge frequently. If you are not happy with the results, allow the paint to dry, then basecoat over the top, sand and start again, or choose other colours. If too much paint collects in the sponge, wring it out, change the water and start again.

Don't be nervous about sponging. You will soon find the right touch. Often the addition of a metallic colour – like gold – will look gorgeous. Don't be modest when painting, if you like a result and you are feeling proud of your efforts then tell yourself how clever you are.

Leather look

In attempting to copy the grains of leather we are permitted a lot of licence, so that really anything goes once you have learned a few techniques. This leather look is a very simple introduction to a multitude of animal skins waiting for you to copy. The surfaces – after tanning – differ greatly. I was very impressed with emu leather.

The technique used is distressing paint with alcohol. This finish is exciting and different. Instructions are given for the 'Leather frame' and the 'Olde leather frame'.

Verdigris

Verdigris is a naturally occurring corrosion on copper and other metals. Painters love to copy this result. Instructions for this finish are given with the 'Musical angels frame' and the 'Distressed daisy frame'.

This finish is ideal for resin frames with moulded designs. For larger frames, some of the paint – like the Iridescent Copper, and even Silver – can be diluted and trickled down the sides. Once again, you are only limited by your imagination. Your admirers will think that age and the elements have produced this effect, especially when you use this technique on large items. This finish is mostly done using a dry brushing technique.

Dry brushing

Dry brushing is a method of applying paint to a surface when we do not want a full coverage like a basecoat. Wisps of paint, to highlight a special effect, are brushed lightly over textured paint. An example of this can be seen on the 'Red & gold frame'.

To practise this technique, put out a little paint on a palette. Using the round or flat chinese brush, pick up a little paint. On a paper towel, work off the paint by going back and forth. Do a little test strip first by whisking very lightly across the ridges or texture. Refer to the 'Baby boy frame' to see how effective this technique is. Both flat and round brushes are useful for dry brushing. Only wash at the end of a project, and wipe off on a paper towel.

Denim

When attempting to copy a material or something that appeals to you, it has to be closely examined, notes taken, ideas and colours jotted down. Copying denim seemed the way to go for a frame for a linedancing friend. Sometimes we have a sample of material or even a photograph to go by.

Denim is not hard to find. If you look at the material, the lines seem to go in a diagonal fashion. The weave is called twill. The stitching is of an orange colour, the seams are double and show signs of wear. We will imitate this by painting diagonally. The technique is mostly dry brushing.

Please refer to the 'Line dancing frame' for full instructions and a step-by-step painting guide.

Patchwork

Patchwork resembles mosaics or inlay. It is a way to use leftover or broken pieces of material, such as timber, stone and ceramics. They are all put together either in a pattern or randomly. This mosaic of material creates a bright and modern frame. This will be a centre of interest in your home. Many materials can be copied. Tartan, for instance, is great to copy, and denim has already been mentioned. Please refer to the 'Patchwork frame'.

Texturing

The application of texture paste to a surface adds another dimension. The texture paste used is acrylic and is applied with a brush or palette knife. Some pastes contain particles that resemble foam or sand and some are plain, but all contain some adherent. Found objects can be set into several of these texture pastes. Please refer to 'Flotsam and jetsam' and 'Gold cherub frame'.

Crackling

Crackling is a magical process. It ages our work and enhances our surfaces. There are two types of crackle medium. There is the sandwich type which goes between layers of paint, and the surface crackle which is applied on top of several layers of paint. The former produces larger cracks and the latter fine cracks which resemble cracked glass when dry.

The more sandwich type medium applied, the larger the cracks. The mediums can be applied with a brush or, for thinner cracks, a small sponge or brush. Instructions are given on the bottle and full instructions are given for the 'Olde crackled frame'. Selective areas were crackled on 'Flotsam & jetsam'. Please refer to the colour plate.

Distressing timber

Distressing timber is great fun to do. It is an aging process and creates another surface of interest.

Today, in furniture shops, you will notice that recycled timbers are often used. New timber can be made to look like this by creating dents and borer holes. To distress new timber you will need; a hammer, nails, a corkscrew, wire, chain and bottle tops. In fact, anything that could make an interesting indentation when it is hammered into wood. Long scratches and grooves can be made with nails.

Assemble a few of the items mentioned and start hammering away, here and there. Don't overdo the hammering. We don't want the frame to break. A small frame will not need as much work as a larger frame.

Some texture paste can also be dragged here and there. The sides of the frames can be distressed, as well. The finish is quite exhilarating. Please refer to the 'Distressed daisy frame' and you will see this effect on the surface when painted.

Lapis lazuli

Lapis lazuli is a semiprecious stone used for ornaments, jewellery and decoration. The largest supplier is Afghanistan. This stone was used in ancient Egypt to decorate coffins, headpieces, etc. It was highly prized and quite expensive, so it was copied.

Depending on the source of supply, colours may vary. It may have more specks and drifts of gold, black and white. When it is polished and if you are fortunate to own a piece, then you might care to copy it. In early times, this stone was ground to a powder and mixed with oils to make a pigment for painting, which was called ultramarine blue. It was a very costly business until paint was artificially produced.

I am sure you will love painting this finish, and full instructions are given for the 'Lapis lazuli frame'. It is a fantasy finish using sponging, spattering, gloss varnishing and reverse glass painting.

Marbling

Marbling is simply an attempt to copy the wonderful polished stone used throughout the world for bathrooms, wall linings, floors, great columns for churches, castles and statuary. Carrara marble from Italy is famous. The statue of David was carved from it. If you wish to copy a particular marble, ceramic and tile showrooms will often sell a tile. Otherwise, copy your own using the various techniques. If you study the marble, you will see that sponging, spattering and liner work all help to replicate this wonderful stone which requires a gloss finish.

Please refer to the 'Green marble frame' to learn how to accomplish this lovely finish.

Tortoiseshell

Tortoiseshell is another finish we like to imitate. Tortoiseshell was first used by the Chinese as an inlay. Europeans loved this effect, and another trade between countries started. The use of this shell is now banned in many countries.

Tortoises and turtles are found in fresh and salt water. Thin slivers are taken from the shell and used as inlay material, made into buttons, combs, fans and shoe horns to name a few.

Today, many items can be found in 'collectables' shops, but modern hair ornaments, etc., are made from plastic. If you want to copy an exact finish, then it can be copied from the real thing or plastic. The fantasy finish has already been explained, and the other techniques are given in the instructions for the small, medium and large tortoiseshell frames. Please refer to the projects.

Fantasy marbling

Fantasy marbling is a quick and delightful way to make a marble finish. To practise this method, put two contrasting colours on a palette; a light and a dark paint. We apply the dark colour as a base colour. Cardboard is a good practice surface. Mix a little of the lighter colour with equal parts of Jo Sonja's 'Faux Finish' Kleister Medium. Have ready several pieces of plastic wrap.

Apply this mix on top and quickly put the plastic over the mix. Push the plastic around and around, then into little pleats. Lift the plastic off and discard. Examine the results. You should have lovely little veins in all directions with the basecoat colour showing through. Dry. Please refer to the 'Baby girl frame'.

If you are feeling a little apprehensive about this, don't be. A coat of Jo Sonja's Clear Glazing Medium can be applied as a barrier in case you want to wipe off the effect, but rarely have I ever seen a result that was not pleasing.

Distressing paint

This can be an aging or modern technique, depending on the end result. The 'Cute teddy frame' is the aged process and the 'Blue dolphin frame' is the modern one. All depends on the underlying layers of paint and the colours of the paints revealed when it is sanded off. Full instructions are given with these frames.

To be effective, the paint needs to be applied fairly thickly so that quite an amount of pressure can be applied when sanding off.

Another method, used on the 'Leather frame', is dabbing on Isopropyl or Rubbing Alcohol. This alcohol will soften the paint and allow it to be worked with a fine stylus to reveal the sub-layer, which creates a new surface effect. Please refer to the 'Leather frame'.

Slip slap

This slip slap way of painting has been explained when varnishing. Another way to slip slap, is to apply paint very thickly, several colours together. You virtually manipulate the paint into ridges which, when dried slowly, keeps these raised areas. This can then be dry brushed with pale gold. I am sure you will love this finish of mine, and there are many other colour combinations waiting to be created by you. Please refer to the 'Red & gold frame' for full instructions. Note that flat brushes are used for this project. For a small frame, $1/4$" is suitable, or a no. 10 roymac shader for the 'Red & gold frame'.

Gold leafing or gilding

This is another fascinating process. If you are using gold leaf for the first time, it is best to work in a draught free area, be quite relaxed and have everything at hand. No heavy breathing!

Gilding, in the past, was a very secretive operation, and it took many years to become a master gilder. Many examples of gilding survive today in large private homes and museums. It remains a very popular pastime and many countries are exporting gold leafed items like fruit, bowls, vases and frames, on paper, clay, wood and leather. Italian leather embossed with gold is well known. In Paris, huge statues have been regilded at a cost of millions of francs for the real thing, and they look glorious.

Tombs and statues were covered with real gold. This was very expensive, so the inexpensive composite fine dutch metal sheets were produced. These are small squares of different fake metals with waxed sheet between each layer. We use this type for the frames. As well as gold we also use silver and an oxidised aluminium type.

Gold leaf is extremely thin but, when glued on with the size, it is quite tough. It can be antiqued and painted. Full instructions are given with the 'Goldleafed mirror' project.

Gold work

The use of gold on our work adds richness and lustre. There are several methods used on our frames and these are seen on the colour plates especially for the 'Wedding frame', 'Gold cherub frame' and the 'Goldleafed mirror'. The uses of different methods are given with each project.

Some surfaces can be painted with metallic powders and glitter mixed with size and paints. These can be difficult to use in confined areas, and a mask should be worn. Our paints, however, are ready mixed and are applied with a nozzle or brush. There is a product called Goldfinger, which is rubbed on with a soft cloth.

Glue-based metallic paints are often used for fabric painting. We use them on our frames. The iridescent paints can be used over the top of paints, to add a little colour and lustre.

While some paints are translucent, we can mix a paint – like Rich Gold, for instance – with water to make this effect. When used over paint such as yellow, the effect is more opaque. Several coats may be needed. Gold spray-paint is another application but hand painting is more enjoyable. Please note that brushes are best cleaned in warm soapy water because the paints may have a glue base. If you are a lover of silver, then just use silver where gold is used.

Dragging

Sometimes in the instructions, I refer to 'dragging the paint'. What this means is that any paint left in a brush – especially after dry brushing – can be dragged down the sides of a frame, rather than working back and forth over a small area. Sometimes two colours are picked up on the brush and lightly dragged down the surface. Please refer to the 'Seaside frame'. The sides of most of the frames are painted in this manner. It makes them more interesting.

Washes

Applying washes over a plain or painted surface adds a soft translucent look. The paint is diluted with water or Jo Sonja's Clear Glazing Medium. Several colours can be washed over one another. The wash must be dry between colours, or a barrier coat of Clear Glazing Medium applied. The wash can be wiped off if you don't like it. Metallic and iridescent colours give a lovely soft glow on the surfaces.

To practise, put out a little paint on a large plate. You will need two jars of water, one for mixing with the paint and the other for cleaning the brush. You will also need a paper towel. I use my large round brush for washes. Only a speck of paint is needed to a puddle of water. Tap off the excess on the paper towel, and apply the diluted paint to the area to be washed. Move the brush around quickly and pick up more wash. It is better to darken as you go. Also, paint out any demarcation lines as you go. Washes dry quickly.

Note that for a pale wash use more water, and for a dark wash use more paint. Washes are used on the 'Olde crackled frame' and on the tortoiseshell finish for the medium and large frames.

Spattering

Spattering has an aging effect and resembles flyspecks. Flicked over our work with an old toothbrush, the small specks soften our painting. Be careful where you spray. You may need to mask off areas, with torn paper towel, where you do not want the spray to go.

To practise on paper, put some dark coloured paint on the palette. Mix with water and the toothbrush. Tap off the excess on a paper towel. Put on a disposable glove. Face the bristles down and run your finger along the bristles where you want the spray to go. Repeat this until you are happy with the results. Should a blob occur, remove it with a cotton bud. But sometimes we love to make blobs and specks. This technique is used in creating the lapis lazuli finish.

Antiquing

Antiquing is a method of aging our work. We apply a darker colour over our painting, then lightly remove it to soften and tone down the colours.

It is possible to purchase special mixes but the following recipe is a good one. It is a water-based mix and, when mixed with Jo Sonja's Retarder & Antiquing Medium, will last for a long time in a jar. The mix is fairly thin. For a thicker mix, more paint to retarder is needed.

A coat of Jo Sonja's Clear Glazing Medium is useful when antiquing for the first time, it acts as a barrier and mistakes can be wiped away. While this glaze coat is drying, prepare the following:
- A small jar with lid
- Jo Sonja's Retarder & Antiquing Medium
- a soft cloth
- cotton buds
- disposable gloves if necessary

for larger areas
- Jo Sonja's Artists Colours
- Raw or Burnt Umber,
- Carbon Black and Turners Yellow.

With a satay stick mix the following together, Twenty parts of Umber to a dash of Carbon Black and Turners Yellow into a jar. Add a little Retarder & Antiquing Medium at a time and mix with the paint until they form a light and creamy consistency.

For small areas use a small brush or the soft cloth. If using a soft cloth, the mix is applied with a soft circular motion. Wipe the mixture over the area, leave for a short time and then wipe off. For heavier antiquing the mix is left on overnight. The retarder will prevent drying out and the surface can be worked. The barrier glaze is needed because more rubbing will be required.

Please refer to the 'Olde leather frame'. Only the corners were antiqued and you will see the mixture in the grooves. It all depends on your taste. The little cotton buds are useful for removing any excess in these grooves.

Set aside to dry for several days, then the frame can be varnished.

Tracing

Tracing is an acceptable way to trace a design onto our frames to paint. Please refer to the black and white designs. If you are intending to paint the 'Distressed daisy frame', please read the following. If you feel that you can paint the design freehand, then please do so.

To trace the design you will need;
- white or grey graphite paper
- some greaseproof paper
- a fine point pen
- a stylus
- a kneadable eraser.

Magic tape can be useful to adhere the tracing. Tracings and graphite can be used over and over again. We use a light graphite on a dark colour paint and a dark graphite on light colours. A kneadable eraser will get rid of graphite lines.

Tear off some greaseproof paper and trace over the black and white design with a fine point pen.

Position this design on the frame with a little magic tape, and slide the graphite paper under it. Note the correct side.

Trace over this design with a satay stick or a stylus. There is no need to put vein lines on the leaves as you will be applying paint there. When painting a face for instance, the face is basecoated and then the facial details traced and painted. The graphite lines are then erased with the kneadable eraser.

Varnishing

Varnishing is the final touch to our work and will protect our painting on the frames. There are many varnishes available, but I would advise using those that are compatible with our folk paints. Namely, Jo Sonja's Water Based Polyurethane Varnish or Acrylic Varnish. Some finishes need only one application, while a gloss finish may need several coats. Some effects like the marble and the lapis lazuli need a gloss finish. Satin varnish is also suitable to protect our work.

A good brush or sponge is essential for varnishing and should be thoroughly cleaned and kept for varnishing only. A little retarder worked into the brush will keep the bristles soft. I like a $1/2$" tacklon brush. When applying several coats in a day, the brush can be wrapped in plastic wrap and cleaned at the end of the day. A hair dryer on a low setting may help dry the varnish between coats.

To varnish, check that the painted frame is dust free and dry. Please read all the instructions and be aware of weather conditions. Put out a little varnish on a lid and load your brush. Work in a criss cross or slip slap fashion over the surface. Hold the frame up to the light to check for ridges and, if there are any, paint them out with a very light sweeping stroke. Just wisp the brush over. Repeat the process until you are happy with the result.

As this is a very important step care needs to be taken so do not hurry the number of coats. Wait as long as possible for the varnish to cure and harden.

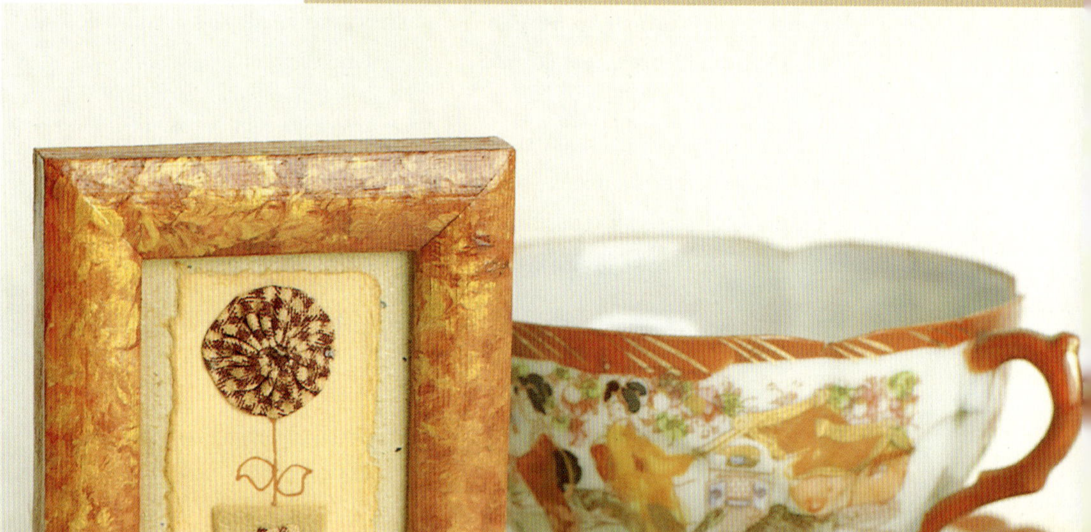

The projects commence with a few easy ones and progress to more advanced techniques. You will have no difficulties if you read through the instructions and the techniques, then note the materials needed for the project you choose.

THE PROJECTS

Fantasy tortoiseshell frame

Fantasy tortoiseshell is a quick and easy way to achieve a very interesting finish. It is fun to do and requires only three tubes of paint and an index finger! Other colour combinations are possible, so please experiment. Have fun.

Techniques
Fantasy tortoiseshell

Requirements
Paints: Jo Sonja's Napthol Crimson, Burgundy, Rich Gold and Pale Gold
Mediums: Jo Sonja's 'Faux Finish' Kleister Medium
Other needs: A satay stick

Procedure

Prepare the frame. Basecoat the frame with Burgundy.

Depending on the size of the frame, put out a small amount of paint and an equal amount of Jo Sonja's 'Faux Finish' Kleister Medium. Mix with the satay stick. Have some paper towels ready to wipe your finger.

Pick up a little Napthol Crimson on your index finger and lightly dab it on the frame. Pick up a little Rich Pale Gold and dab it near the Napthol Crimson, then a dab of Burgundy, then Gold and Crimson. Go round the frame in this way.

The Kleister Medium will make little mounds of paint, and you will see your fingerprints in the paint. This is what we want to see. The medium and paint mix will dry flat and leave this interesting finger finish. Small decorative buttons can be used to create designs too.

Apply two coats of satin or gloss varnish.

Seaside frame

This frame – a timber one – contained a seaside scene that I liked, so I painted the frame to match the picture. It often happens that we have a painting but do not like the frame, or it does not match our décor. We can choose our own colours, prepare and repaint the frame and be happy with the results.

Techniques
Sponging, texturing, dry brushing, varnishing

Requirements
Paints: Jo Sonja's Light Ultramarine Blue, Titanium White, Yellow Ochre, Gold Oxide, Moss Green, Burgundy, Dioxin Purple

Brushes: No. 5 round, an old one if possible or a chinese brush

Other needs: A sea sponge, Deco Art's 'Sandstone' Natural Beige

Procedure
Prepare the frame and seal it. Apply two coats of Yellow Ochre to the entire frame.

Refer to the sponging instructions. Put out small dabs of all the paints and using the dampened sponge, pick up the paint and work in little drifts of colour here and there. Not too much Dioxin Purple or Burgundy. Refer to the painting, or scene, and add more colour if needed. The back of the frame can be used for practice. If you are not happy with the result, sand off and apply more Yellow Ochre.

Allow to dry, then gloss varnish.

36

With the old brush, thickly apply the Deco Art 'Sandstone' Natural Beige around the outer moulded edge. This will take some time to dry, possibly overnight. More texture may be needed here and there, but it must be completely dry before moving to the next stage. Drag some texture over the sides of the frame, too.

Dry brush Titanium White over the top. Mix a little Titanium White with a little Light Ultramarine Blue to make a pale blue, and dry brush here and there. Stand your work up, stand back and admire it, or apply more paint. Well done.

The back of the frame can be used for practice. If you are not happy with the [...] sand off and [...] re Yellow Ochre.

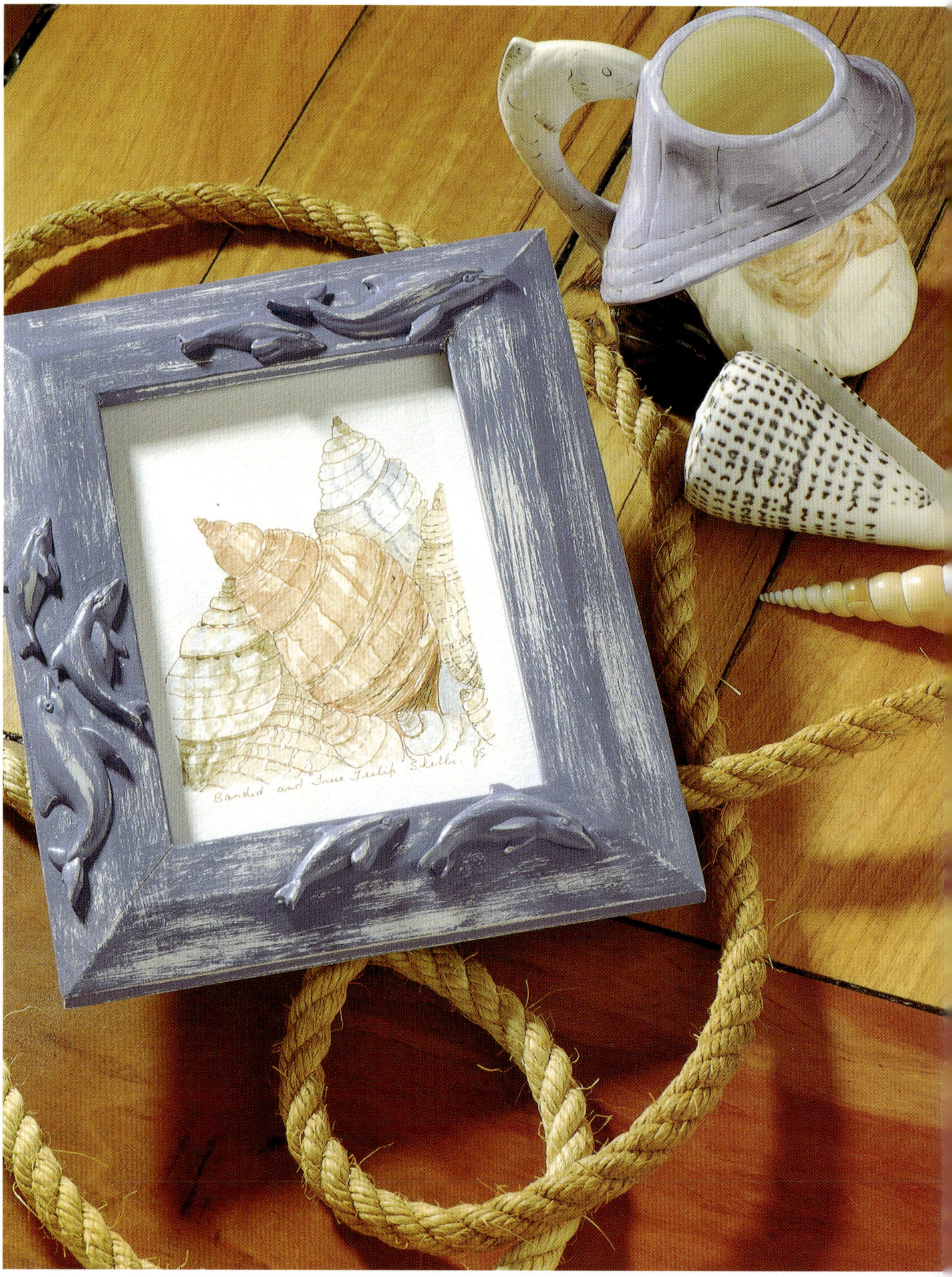
Banded and True Tulip Shells.

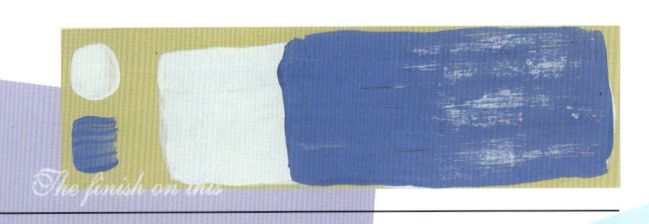

Blue dolphin frame

The finish on this frame resembles the 'milk finish' on old furniture. The plastic dolphins were found in a discount shop. It is a quick and easy frame to paint.

Techniques
Distressing paint

Requirements
Paints: Jo Sonja's Blue Sapphire or Azure Blue, Warm White
Brushes: Basecoat
Other needs: Fine and course sandpaper, packet of plastic dolphins, craft glue

Procedure
Prepare the frame and seal. Most sealers have an adhesive base so I glued the dolphins on with this. Otherwise you need to use a water-based glue, like Aquadhere. Other glues might come off if they are dampened with paint. Allow the glue to dry overnight and then apply sealer to the dolphins.

Apply two coats of Warm White over the whole frame. Apply one coat of sealer over this white. Apply one or two coats of blue over the white.

When dry, fold a small piece of the course sandpaper and rub it over the paintwork, here and there, until some of the white shows through. Sand in an up and down direction. Apply more pressure to reveal more of the white underneath. Stop when you are happy with the result. Fold a piece of the fine sandpaper and sand until you have a smooth surface. Dust off and apply two coats of satin varnish.

This colour combination makes a lovely frame for a modern home or for dolphin lovers.

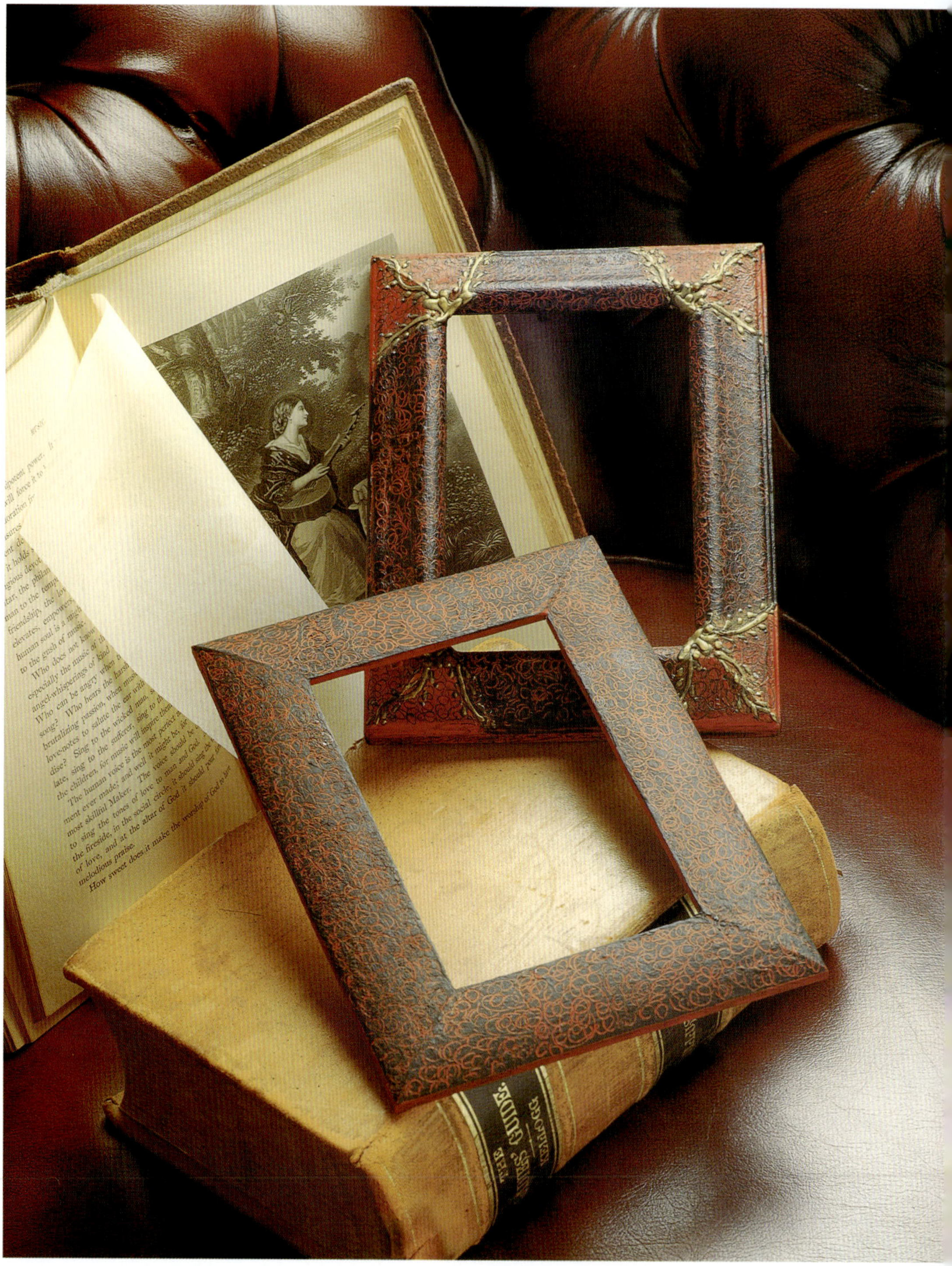

Leather frame

See line illustration page 96

This is a delight to paint, your friends will want to pick it up and feel it.

Techniques
Leather look, distressing paint

Requirements
Paints: Jo Sonja's Carbon Black, Napthol Crimson
Brushes: No. 5 round or chinese brush
Medium: Rubbing or Isopropyl Alcohol from supermarket or chemist
Other needs: Fine point stylus, paper towel, small container, fine sandpaper

Procedure
Prepare the frame and apply three thick coats of Napthol Crimson to the front and sides. Apply one coat of Carbon Black to the back of the frame.

When dry, apply one thick coat of Carbon Black over the Napthol Crimson.

Put a little alcohol in the small container and apply some to a small area of the frame with the brush. Wait a few seconds and then, with the end of the stylus, check to see if the paint has softened, then go round and round making small circles. The Napthol Crimson will be revealed and you will see the design. Add more alcohol, wait a few seconds and repeat the process. You can only do a small area at a time. You will find that the alcohol dries quickly if you get too far ahead. If the paint won't lift, apply more alcohol, wait and try again. From time to time wipe the paint off the stylus onto a paper towel. Do the sides as well.

When dry, brush off any excess paint or very lightly sand, then apply gloss or satin varnish.

This is a stunning finish. Often when we are painting a project, other ideas will pop into our head. Jot these ideas down on paper, so they are not forgotten.

Olde leather frame

This frame has the same finish as the last frame except for the corners that have the paint colours reversed. The addition of some dimensional gold paint, which is antiqued, makes for a most interesting frame. These finishes are ideal for the men in your life.

Techniques
Distressing paint, antiquing, leather look

Requirements
Paints: Jo Sonja's Napthol Crimson, Carbon Black
Brushes: No. 5 round or chinese brush
Medium: Alcohol, Jo Sonja's Retarder & Antiquing Medium
Dimensional paint: Plaid Fashion Fabric Paint's Pure Gold
Other needs: Fine point stylus, pencil, cotton bud

Procedure

Please read the instructions and the process for the Leather frame. For the corner design please refer to the black and white design and colour picture to see where the black basecoat goes, then the red on top. Mark with a pencil if necessary, apply paint and distress.

When the excess paint has been brushed off, wipe the frame and apply the dimensional paint on the corners. If using these paints for the first time, practise on paper. Do not squeeze too hard. It is better to wipe off any mistakes and start again, touching up when dry. Allow to dry overnight.

To antique the gold point; make up a small amount of the mix and apply with a cotton bud, wipe off gently until you like the result. Allow to dry and then varnish with satin or gloss finish.

Musical angels frame

This little resin frame was bought in a discount shop. If you can't find one, then shapes can be glued on. Refrigerator magnets are interesting and the variety is endless.

Techniques
Verdigris, dry brushing, slip slap

Requirements
Paints: Jo Sonja's Aqua, Sapphire, Yellow Light, Rich Gold, Warm White, Raw Umber, Copper Iridescent

Brushes: 1/4" flat, no. 3 round or chinese brushes

Mediums: Jo Sonja's Clear Glazing Medium

Procedure

Basecoat the frame with Aqua. On the palette, put out small amounts of Sapphire, Aqua, Yellow Light and Warm White. Firstly, slip slap some Sapphire and then Aqua over the frame and the angels. Apply one coat of Jo Sonja's Clear Glazing Medium over this when it is dry. This acts as a barrier and you can remove excess paint or any mistakes with cotton buds.

Dry brush a little Yellow Light here and there. As the frame is small, these little areas of colour will be small too. Brush over the hair, border and instruments.

Dry brush a little Warm White on top and close to the Yellow Light, and then drag some Warm White around the borders and sides of the frame. Apply a coat of Clear Glazing Medium,

44

and dry. Hint: Use one brush for basecoating and glazing. You can wsh that brush. Use the other brush for drybrushing and simply wipe it clean – don't wet it.

Put out a little Rich Gold and Iridescent Copper, and dry brush some other areas with these colours. If at any stage you feel you have overdone one colour, you can always paint over the top with a little Aqua or Sapphire and start again. Apply a coat of Clear Glazing Medium over this.

To shade, mix a little Raw Umber with water and trickle it down with a brush into some of the little crevices. This will also age the shapes and finish. Check the finish. There does need to be some white showing to resemble the powder that dries on the copper. Sometimes verdigris appears to be very bright green and silvery. The addition of these colours can be pleasing, too.

When dry, apply satin varnish.

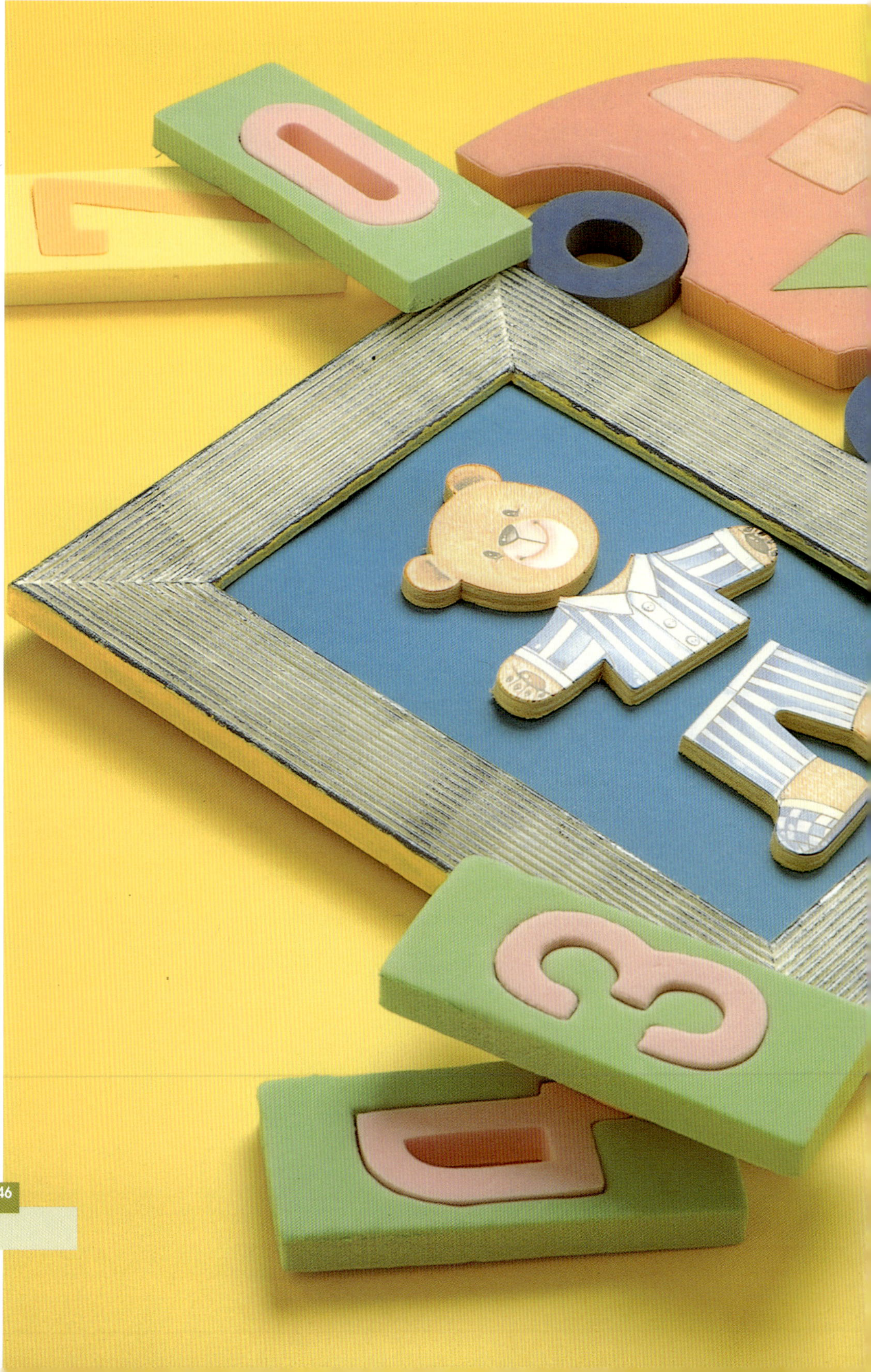

Baby boy frame

This grooved timber frame presented a challenge, so dry brushing seemed to be the way to go. I found a small teddy bear which responded to the same technique

Techniques
Dry brushing

Requirements
Paints: Jo Sonja's Sapphire, Titanium White, Yellow Light, Pearl White
Brushes: Basecoat, a chinese brush
Other needs: Paper towels, craft glue, fine blue or pink ribbon, a resin teddy bear

Procedure
Basecoat the frame with three coats of Titanium White, getting down into all the grooves. Dry brush with Sapphire across the ridges. Drag some Yellow Light down the sides of the frame.

Remove magnet from the bear and basecoat the bear with Yellow Light. Allow to dry. Dry brush across the ridges with Titanium White, and dry. Dry brush Pearl White over the Titanium White. This will give a shiny effect. Drag a little Pearl White down the sides of the frame. Apply one coat of satin varnish.

Tie a fine blue ribbon around the neck of the bear. Glue the bear onto the frame with strong craft glue. Please refer to the colour plate.

This makes an ideal gift for a new baby. Should it be for a girl then use pink instead of blue.

48

Line dancing frame

Line dancing is very popular today, and I was given a photo to frame. Trying to copy denim was great fun. The little gold ornaments are available in craft shops.

Techniques
Denim, dry brushing, liner brush work

Requirements
Paints: Jo Sonja's Storm Blue, Smoked Pearl, Warm White, Gold Oxide

Brushes: No. 5 round or a chinese brush, fine liner brush

Other needs: P.V.C. wood glue (Aquadhere), 1 metre (3') of $1/2$ cm ($1/4$") white cotton cord, scissors

Mediums: Jo Sonja's Clear Glazing Medium

Procedure
Basecoat the frame Storm Blue. Apply one coat of Jo Sonja's Clear Glazing Medium.

Mix a little Storm Blue with Smoked Pearl to make a nice denim blue. Dry brush this colour diagonally across the frame. When dry, dry brush in the opposite direction diagonally, making an 'X'. Apply one coat of Clear Glazing Medium.

Dry brush some Smoked Pearl over these areas. Apply one coat of Clear Glazing Medium.

Dry brush some Warm White over these areas. If you look at denim, little patches appear here and there that look worn, so repeat the colours until you like the effect.

The corners of the frame are seams. Please refer to the colour plate. Make a fine line in each corner with Storm Blue. Add fine dashes with Gold Oxide, to resemble stitching.

Measure the cord and cut the ends diagonally. Glue the cord evenly around the outside of the frame, using P.V.C. wood glue and a chinese brush. A hair dryer is useful here to speed the drying time of the glue. Apply more glue over the cord and let it dry overnight. The glue hardens the cord and dries clear.

When the cord is dry, apply two coats of Smoked Pearl. Dry brush with Warm White. With the fine liner brush and Gold Oxide, paint some fine strokes in between the twists of the cord.

Apply gloss varnish. The metal shapes are glued on with craft glue.

Patchwork frame

You might have a sample of your first patchwork, or an antique piece of material or lace, but whatever is intended

The mosaic effect of different materials is bright and cheery. You might have a sample of your first patchwork, or an antique piece of material or lace, but whatever is intended for this frame, a ridged cardboard backing is more attractive than mat board. The frame needs to have a border and a fairly wide inner border for the design.

Technique
Patchwork, dots, comma strokes, varnishing

Requirements
Paints: Jo Sonja's Yellow Light, Napthol Crimson, Titanium White, Sapphire, Green Oxide, Burgundy, Brown Earth

Brushes: Fine liner, no. 3, no. 5 round

Other needs: A stylus, carbon pencil, black pen, fine point no. 1 Artline Drawing System, Magic Tape

Procedure
Basecoat the frame with three coats of Titanium White.

Draw material shapes with a pencil. The painting for the material is all freehand. It is best to work around the frame and mask off each colour as you go. This makes the material joins appear neater. A hair dryer will make the job easier.

Paint the background colours first and then decorate. For instance, for the yellow material, it would be advisable to put out the Napthol Crimson,

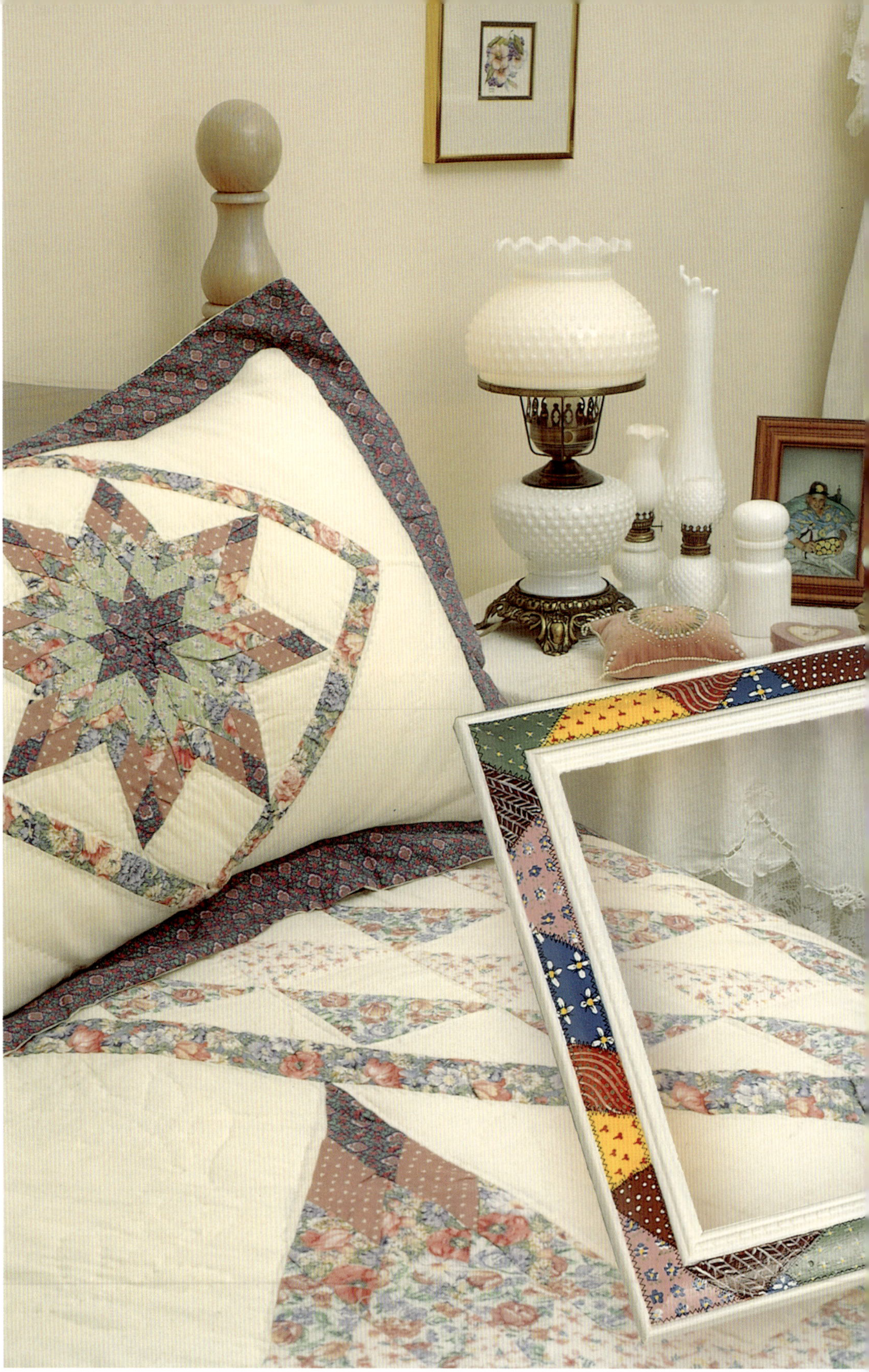

make two dots with the stylus, pull down the centre into a heart shape and go on to the next yellow piece. Please refer to the pattern guide and paint the rest of the materials.

The pink colour is made with a tiny dab of Napthol Crimson to the Titanium White until a nice pink is blended. When dry, put out Sapphire and Titanium White and, using the small round brush, pick up a little of each colour on the tip of the brush and push five small petals to make a flower. A small yellow dot made with the stylus is placed in the centre. Put out a little Green Oxide and with the fine liner brush make small ticks for leaves around these flowers.

The white daisies are four small comma strokes painted in the shape of a cross with the no. 3 round brush. When dry, apply a large yellow dot. Keep referring to the colour worksheet and make dots and fine lines.

When completely dry, and using the fine point pen, draw zigzag lines between all the materials and the edge of the frame to resemble stitching. Draw stamens in the daisies and decorate with the black pen.

Allow at least 24 hours for the pen work to dry before gloss varnishing the frame.

Well done, especially if you have never painted before.

This heavily textured frame resembles old plaster w...
grime. Plaster was cast into moulds and set onto ce...
painted. Today, a texture paste is used and found o...
These found objects can be a mixture of odd things ...
found, fern, coins, fishing line, cord, plastic stars, m...
buttons and screws. The knotted cord made the fra...
tremendous amount of fun making this frame.

Flotsam
& jetysam

This heavily textured frame resembles old plaster work aged with smoke and years of grime. Plaster was cast into moulds and set onto ceilings and walls then whitewashed or painted. Today, a texture paste is used and found objects are set into this glue-based paste.

These found objects can be a mixture of odd things or a collection of one item, like shells. I found, fern, coins, fishing line, cord, plastic stars, mesh, torn sponge, wood, fish hooks, beads, buttons and screws. The knotted cord made the frame appear nautical. I had a tremendous amount of fun making this frame. A great frame for dad.

Techniques
Texturing, dry brushing, crackling

Requirements
Paints: Jo Sonja's Raw Umber, Titanium White, Red Earth
Brushes: No. 5 round or a chinese brush
Medium: Jo Sonja's Décor Crackle
Other needs: Deco Art's Sparkling 'Sandstone' in a pale colour

Procedure
Have the found objects washed, dried and ready to apply. Apply the Art Deco Sparkling 'Sandstone' around the frame. Push the objects into the 'Sandstone' and, when you are happy with the result, set it aside to dry overnight or longer if necessary.

When it is dry and the objects are immovable, apply two coats of Titanium White, getting into all the little grooves and indentations. When dry apply some Jo Sonja's Décor Crackle to some of the areas you think are too plain. Refer to the crackling instructions on the 'Olde crackled frame' project. Allow the Décor Crackle to dry.

Mix some Red Earth to a nice creamy consistency and paint it over the frame, taking care where you applied the Décor Crackle. Note the instant result. When this coat is dry, apply another coat of Red Earth, except where the crackling is. Drag some of this colour along the sides of the frame. Drag a little Titanium White and Raw Umber, too. Examine the frame and if you would like to dry brush a little Titanium White here and there, please do so.

Dilute a little Raw Umber with water. With the round brush, trickle some of this darker mix in between some of the objects, for shading. Apply one coat of satin varnish.

Well that's it for dad, I hope he appreciated all your hard work and imagination.

Olde cracked frame

An old postcard, similar to the one in the 'Distressed daisy frame', was the inspiration for this frame. The crackling procedure is fun, and I received a lot of pleasure and satisfaction from completing such a frame.

Techniques
Crackling, washes, dry brushing

Requirements
Paints: Jo Sonja's Plum Pink, Unbleached Titanium, Silver, Dioxin Purple, Green Light, Rich Gold, Sapphire
Brushes: $1/2$" basecoat, no. 5 round, small sponge
Medium: Jo Sonja's Décor Crackle

Procedure
Mix a nice lavender colour with 1 part Dioxin Purple to 10 parts Unbleached Titanium. Apply this mix to the larger border. Two coats may be needed.

Apply two coats of Sapphire to the inner moulding.

Please read the instructions for crackling before proceeding. Note that the cracks in the paint are wider on the border and finer on the inner moulding. Apply the Jo Sonja's Décor Crackle on the border with a $1/2$" brush, fairly thickly. Apply the Décor Crackle on the moulding with a sponge, fairly lightly. Set the frame aside to dry. A hair dryer may be useful here.

Using the $1/2$" brush, mix a large creamy mix of Unbleached Titanium and apply fairly thickly over the Décor Crackle. Using the

Magnolia

[MAGNOLIA ACUMINATA]

no. 5 brush, apply the paint less thickly on the inner moulding. If the paint drags, leave it for a while and start again. Apply in one direction only on the outer border.

By this time you will notice lovely cracks appearing. Go over any missed spots. Set the frame aside to dry.

When the frame is completely dry, mix a wash of Plum Pink and water. Apply the wash with the large brush around the edge of the moulding and frame.

Make a wash of Rich Gold and water, and apply it over the frame. When dry, drag a little Rich Gold along the sides of the frame and dry brush some gold paint over the washes here and there.

Make a wash of Green Light and apply it to the moulding. Add more paint to the water if you prefer a darker colour. Dry brush some Silver around the inner border, still allowing the other colours to show through.

Apply one coat of satin varnish.

Assemble the frame. If you are using this frame for an old card, there are many decorative and hand made papers on the market that will show off the card. As this frame will hang on the wall, there are some lovely cords, velvet and wired ribbon available. These can be glued or stapled onto the back of the frame.

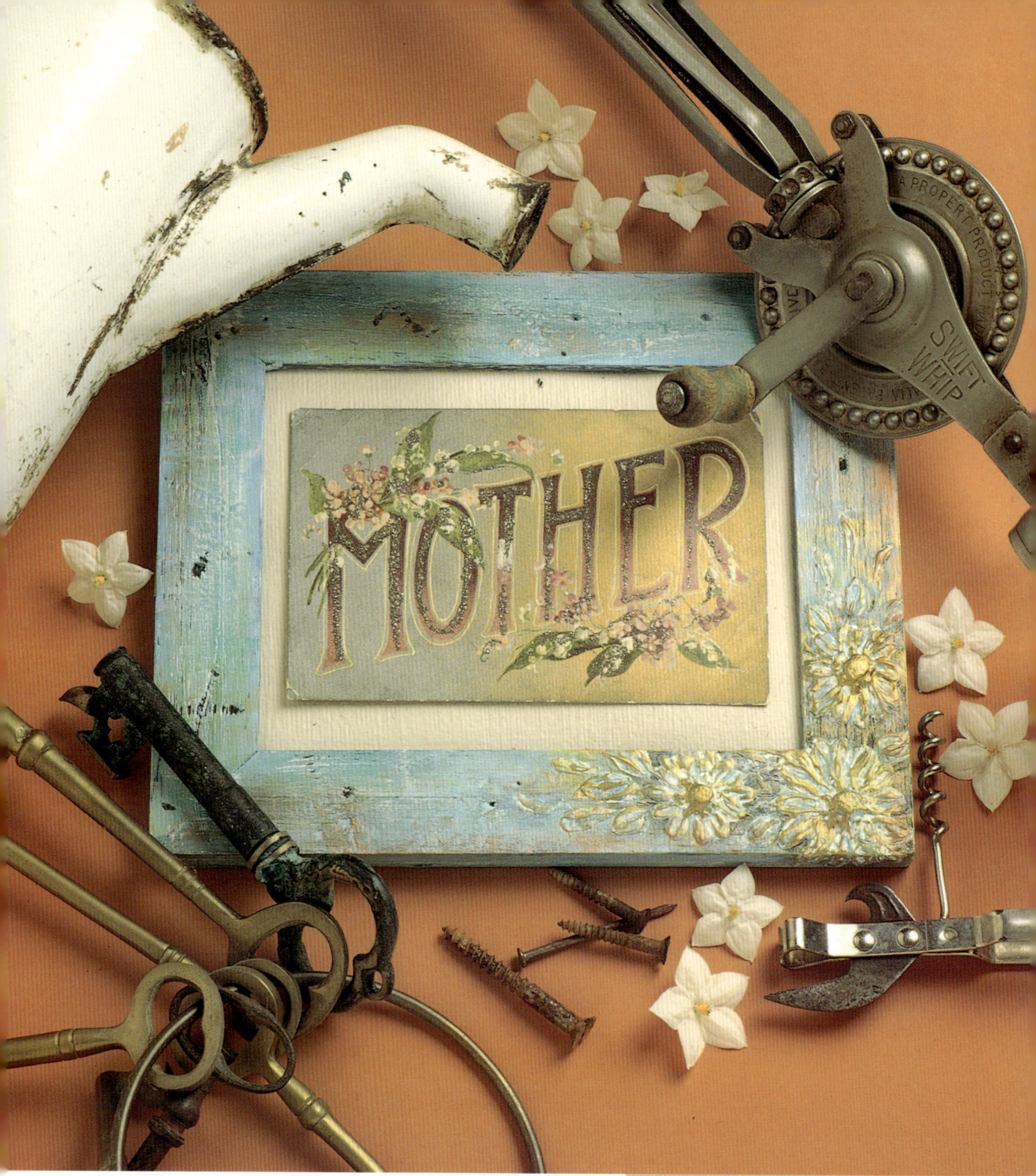
MOTHER
SWIFT WHIP

Distressed daisy frame

See line illustration page 96

Many of our decorative painting texhniques deliberately 'age' our painting. Distressing timber is one way. An old postcard is ideal for this frame, just pick out a colour that appeals to you and paint the frame to match.

Techniques

Distressing timber, texturing, dry brushing, round brush comma strokes, tracing, slip slap

Requirements

Paints:	Jo Sonja's Aqua, Sapphire, Rich Gold, Raw Umber, Warm White, Copper Iridescent
Brushes:	No. 4 round, $1/4$" flat, a chinese brush
Mediums:	Jo Sonja's Texture Paste
Other needs:	Tracing paper or carbon pencil, white graphite paper, stylus or satay stick

Procedure

Sand and seal the frame. Then distress the frame. You could make some grooves with nails dragged down the timber, add some texture paste and sand with rough sandpaper. This is a marvellous way to take out any frustrations we might have, on the frame. Full instructions for distressing timber are given in the 'Techniques & finishes' section. It is not necessary to distress the area where the design will go.

When the paste is dry, mix a little Raw Umber with water and, using the round brush, paint into the grooves and indentations.

Slip slap some Aqua, then Sapphire, around the frame and sides with the $1/4$" brush.

Dry brush some Warm White here and there, and then dry brush Rich Gold followed by Copper Iridescent here and there.

Apply one coat of satin varnish.

Trace the daisy design (or draw it freehand) with the carbon pencil. White graphite paper is probably the best paper to trace onto the blue/green colour.

Paint the petals with Jo Sonja's Texture Paste using the no. 4 round brush. You will discover – when you paint the petals in a comma stroke with the Texture Paste – that there is a groove down the centre of the paste. This is normal. When dry, apply another coat to build-up the petals. The centre of each daisy is a circle of thick paste. When almost dry, make holes in the centre with the stylus or satay stick. Our work here does not have to be perfect. Drag some Texture Paste onto the sides, and dry brush Warm White, Gold and Copper. The leaves are just small groups of strokes like the painted petals.

When the design is quite dry, apply Aqua over the daisies and leaf strokes. When dry, dry brush with Rich Gold and touch up here and there with Copper Iridescent. The painted finish is similar to verdigris.

Mix a little Raw Umber with water and – using the round brush – paint a few little shadows around the daisies and leaves.

This frame will hang well so a nice gold cord or a gold tassel would complement your lovely frame.

Wedding frame

See line illustration page 96

This charming frame would enhance any wedding photo. It would make a lovely gift for the parents of the bride and groom, or a surprise gift which the bride or groom has painted for framing their favourite photo of the big day.

It is quick and easy to paint and makes use of dimensional, metallic and iridescent paints. The little angels were found in a craft shop.

Techniques
Sponging, dry brushing, gold work

Requirements
Paints: Jo Sonja's Rich Gold, Pale Gold, Green, Red and Purple Iridescent, Yellow Oxide, Warm White

Brushes: Basecoat, no. 4 round

Other needs: Plaid Fashion Fabric Paint's Pure Gold (in a bottle with applicator), little angels, sea sponge, craft glue, carbon pencil, cotton bud

Procedure
Prepare the frame and apply one or two coats of Yellow Oxide over the whole frame. Apply one coat of Pale Gold over this. Sponge Pale and Rich Gold lightly over this. When dry, sponge drifts of Red, Green then Purple Iridescent, here and there. One or more applications of these last three paints may be needed. On this particular frame with the bands on the inner mouldings, they were then painted with alternate Rich then Pale Gold. The frame should glow.

Apply two coats of gloss varnish and dry. Please refer to the colour.

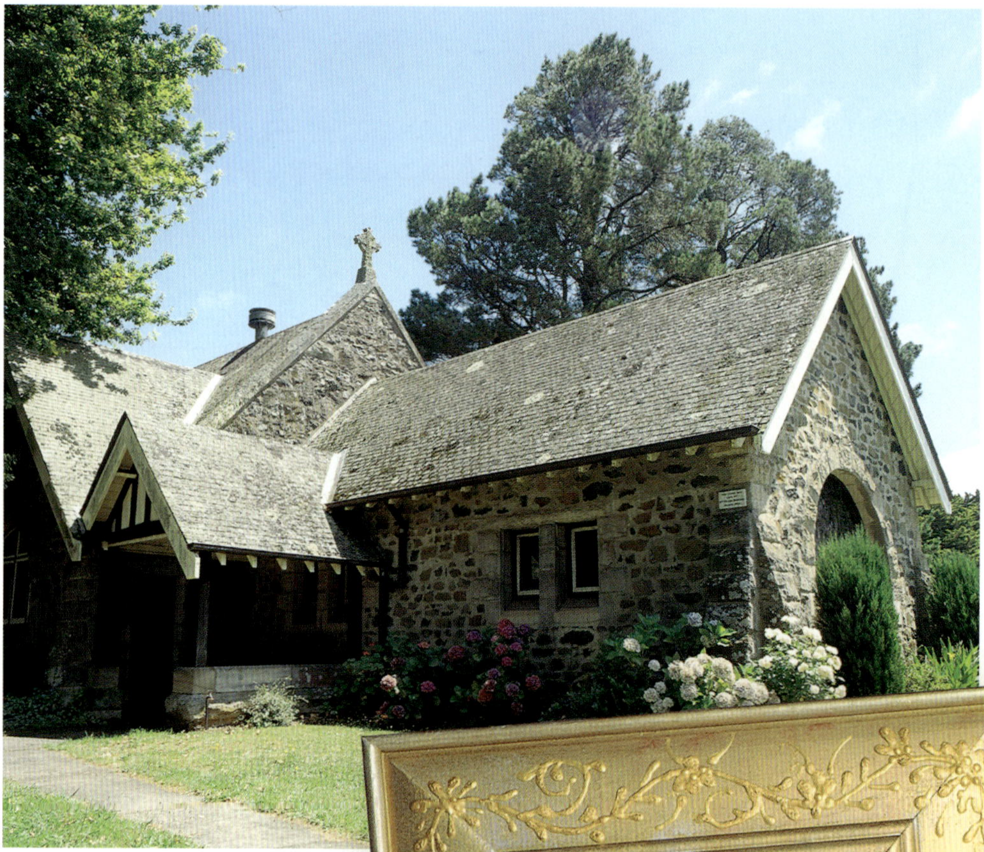

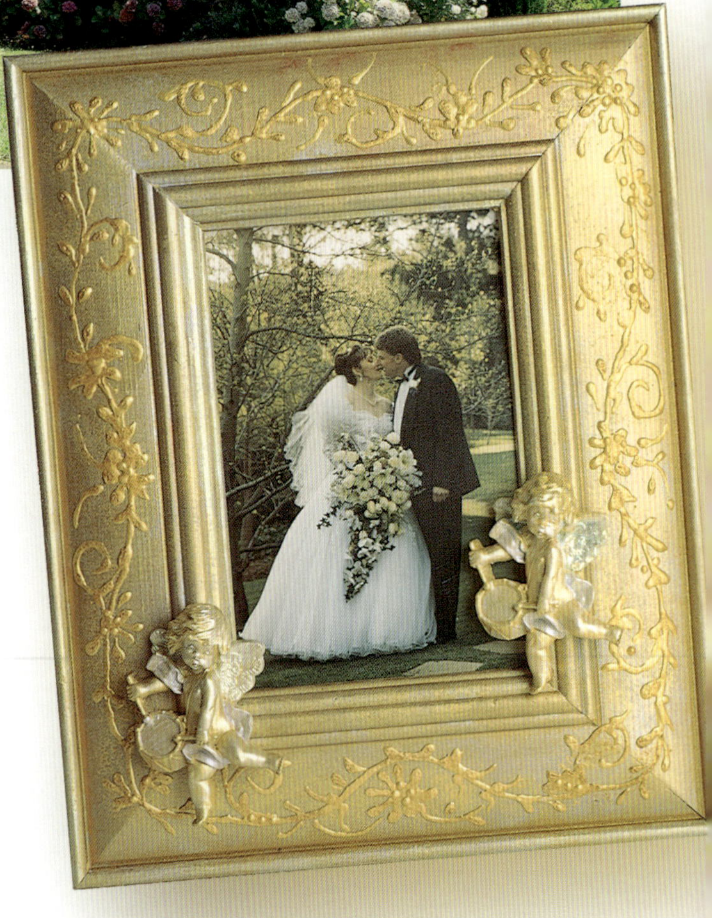

You are now ready to apply the Plaid Fashion Fabric's Pure Gold fabric paint. Pencil in the main curves of the design and work closely to the design. Check on a paper towel that you can move the paint while you are squeezing it out through the nozzle. It is best to work away from you and work in one direction so you don't smudge the paint. At first it is best to apply a thin line and – when dry – go back over the line again. The drying time for this paint is overnight. Remove any mistakes with a cotton bud.

The flowers, leaves and buds are all comma strokes. To take away from the plainness of this paint, I suggest that before it is completely dry, you tap the paint very lightly with a textured sponge. It really creates a nice soft finish.

When completely dry, dry brush some Rich Gold here and there. Squeeze some dots in the centres of the flowers and along the stems.

The little angels were basecoated with two coats of Warm White and, when dry, one was painted with Rich Gold and the other Pale Gold. Two coats may be needed. Dry brush Rich Gold on the hair of the Pale Gold angel and on the drums, etc., and dry brush Pale Gold on some of the Rich Gold angel. Apply several coats of Red, Green and Purple on the draping, the drums, etc. Glue these onto the frame with strong craft glue.

You should be very proud of this frame you have painted. Great effort!

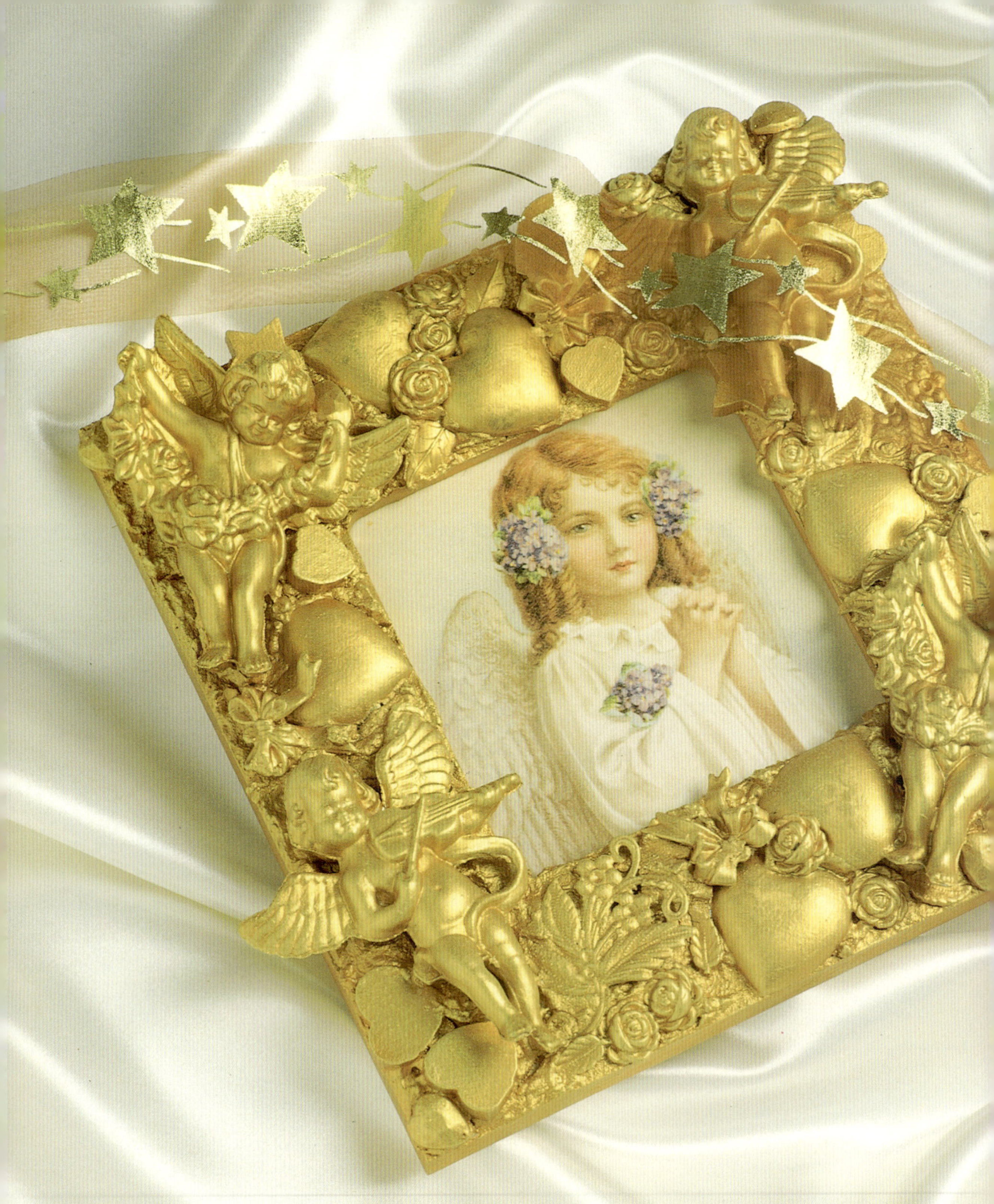

Gold cherub frame

This stunning square frame is designed to give to someone you love. It is quick to paint once you have found the angels and all the little bits and pieces. I found the angels floating around in the supermarket. I found the little rose buttons, wood pieces, plastic and metal shapes in craft shops. I tend to buy interesting pieces knowing that one day they will come in handy for something, and they did!

Techniques
Gold work, dry brushing, texturing

Requirements
Paints: Jo Sonja's Rich Gold and Pale Gold

Brushes: Round, flat, a chinese brush

Other needs: Deco Art Sparkling 'Sandstone', a pale colour if possible

Procedure
Prepare the frame. Have all the little bits and pieces set out. Apply the Deco Art Sparkling 'Sandstone' very thickly on the frame and drag a little on the sides. Push the items into this mix, adding more sandstone paint if necessary. Fill up any little spaces with more items until you are happy with the result. Set aside to dry, this may

take 24 hours or more, depending on the weather.

Apply one generous coat of sealer over this. It also acts as a glue.

Apply two or more coats of Rich Gold, getting down into all the little grooves. When dry, dry brush some Pale Gold over some of raised areas here and there. Apply one coat of satin varnish.

The back and sides of the frame will need to be painted gold too.

This frame resembles the very expensive gold leafed frames. Perhaps, later on – when you have learnt to use gold leaf – you might want to gild a frame such as this. It would be a lot of work, but very rewarding.

Lapis lazuli frame

This particular frame was chosen because of the size of the glass and the narrow border. This allows me to describe the reverse glass painting technique and the normal way to paint lapis lazuli with the outcome the same.

When viewed from the other side, the finish resembles the high glossy finish of decoupage. Here the glass takes on the appearance of varnish. On the border the opposite occurs and we apply the glossy finish.

My print was a copy of gold work that was embroidered by the royal school of needleworkers.

Techniques
Lapis lazuli, spattering, sponging, liner work

Requirements
Paints: Jo Sonja's Rich Gold and Pale Gold, Ultramarine Blue, Burgundy, Yellow Oxide, Carbon Black, Titanium White, Aqua, Dioxin Purple

Brushes: Fine liner, an old toothbrush, basecoat

Mediums: Jo Sonja's Clear Glazing Medium Jo Sonja's All Purpose Sealer

Other needs: A small textured sponge, Magic Tape, a container of water, saucer or plate, a disposable glove, hair dryer

Procedure
Cut a piece of paper the size of your card or print. Measure, and centre this cutout with folds of masking tape under the paper. Apply one coat of Jo Sonja's All Purpose Sealer on the glass. When

70

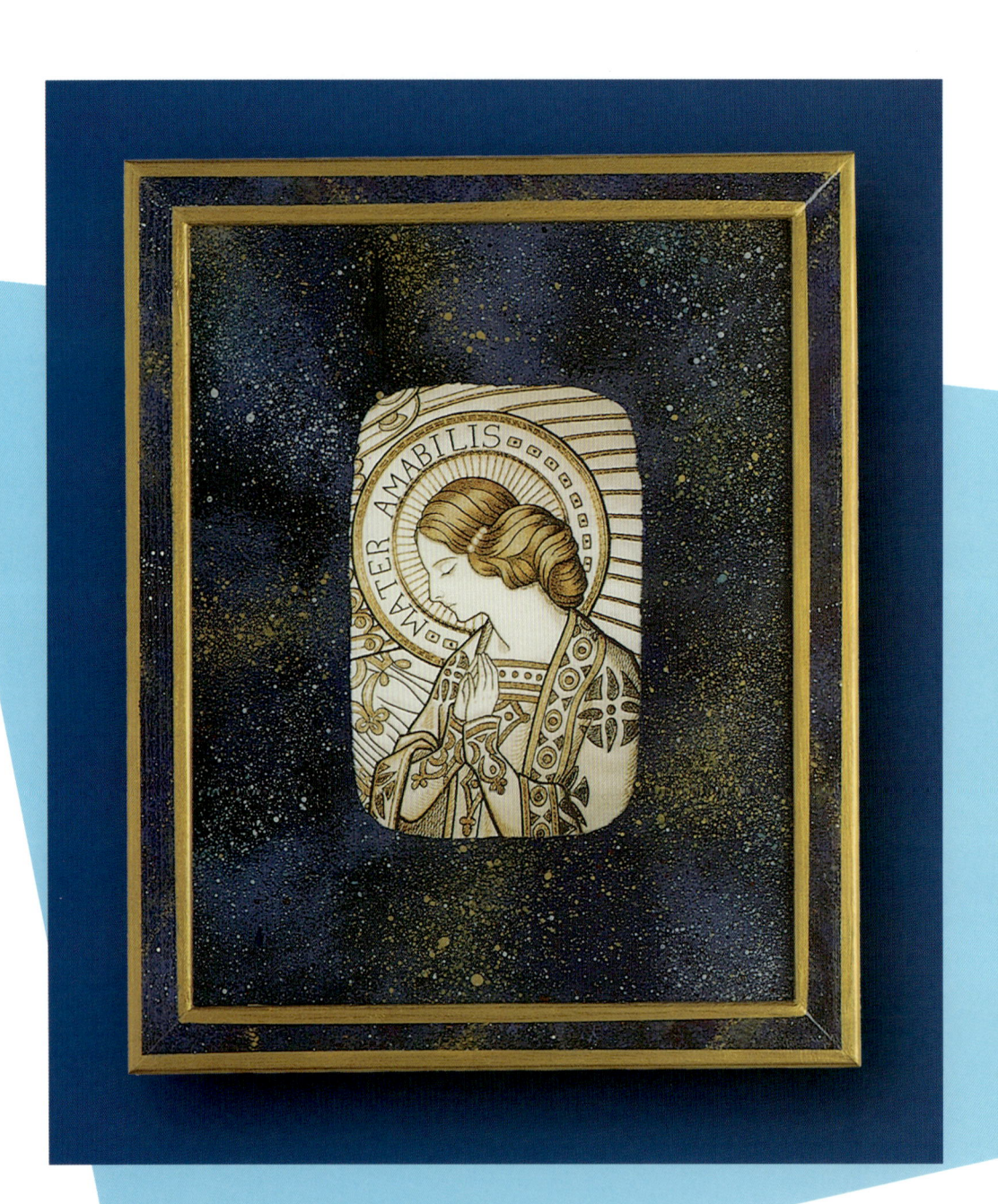

applying paint around this paper, just press down the edges to prevent bleeding. A small scraper will remove any mistakes, though.

Note that paint must be dry between colour applications. If you are in doubt about a colour or you may have applied too much paint, a coat of Jo Sonja's Clear Glazing Medium between colours allows paint to be removed. It acts as a barrier between the coats. The Glazing Medium also gives a 'tooth' for the paint to adhere to.

Make the glass and surrounding area ready for spattering. A disposable glove is handy here as well as a hair dryer on a cool setting. Mix the paints with a little water. Tap off the excess on a paper towel and run your finger along the bristles of the toothbrush, where you want the spray to go. Pick up more paint on the toothbrush if necessary. Wash out the brush between colours.

Spatter some Titanium White here and there. Spatter some Rich Gold and Pale Gold here and there in little drifts and dry between colour changes. Spatter some Yellow Oxide near the gold spattering. Spatter a very small spray of Dioxin Purple here and there. Spatter a little Burgundy near the Purple. Spatter a little Aqua here and there. Apply some Clear Glazing Medium over this.

Turn the glass over and see what is happening. If more spattering is needed, apply more before the sponging takes place. Refer to the colour plate.

Wring out the sponge in water, and gently sponge on some Ultramarine Blue in several areas. Again, turn the glass over and check what is happening and where more sponging may be needed before the black is applied. Once you have sponged you can't apply more spattering.

Gently sponge on the Carbon Black. Examine again and sponge on perhaps a little Aqua or Burgundy in any little gaps, or just the Ultramarine Blue. The glass now has solid paint over the spattering. Apply one coat of Clear Glazing Medium and set aside to dry. Remove the paper cutout and scrape off any paint that has bled under it.

Now for the frame. Apply one coat of yellow oxide. When dry, apply a strip of Magic Tape down the middle and paint the small borders Rich Gold. When dry, apply Magic Tape over these borders and in the centre space we will start the opposite process of lapis lazuli on glass.

Sponge on a little Carbon Black here and there. When dry, sponge on some Ultramarine Blue and a little Burgundy, covering the basecoat colour. Apply a coat of Clear Glazing Medium

Spatter some Burgundy, then Ultramarine Blue, then Dioxin Purple. Spatter in drifts. Apply more of the Clear Glazing Medium and dry between colours. The opposite is happening here now. Spatter Gold Oxide in drifts and – near here – spatter some Rich Gold. Compare the finish with the glass and apply more spattering if necessary. The last spattering is of Titanium White,

here and there. When dry, remove the tape and touch up any little spots on the borders with Rich Gold.

The next step is to varnish. We need a high-gloss finish, so five or six coats may be needed to obtain this finish. A light sanding with wet and dry paper may be needed after two coats of varnish.

I do hope you enjoyed painting this lapis lazuli finish. Replicating other stones – such as granite, marble and porphyry – is not difficult, once you know the techniques.

Replicating other stones — such as granite, marble and porphyry — is not difficult, once you know the techniques.

Green marble frame

Marble comes in a wide range of colours. If you need an exact match, look at some marble and write a list of the colours you see. For this finish to be effective, the frame needs to have a minimum width of 4 cm (1 $^1/_2$").

Traditionally, goose feathers were used for making vein lines in marble so you might have to go feather hunting. I have a collection of feathers from cockatoos to budgies. However, a liner brush does the job just as well. The sides of the frame were marbled too.

Techniques
Fantasy marbling, sponging, spattering, varnishing

Requirements
Paints: Jo Sonja's Moss Green, Green Oxide, Carbon Black, Smoked Pearl, Pale Gold
Brushes: Fine liner, old toothbrush, no. 5 round, a large brush for pouncing
Mediums: Rubbing alcohol, Jo Sonja's Clear Glazing Medium, Jo Sonja's 'Faux Finish' Kleister Medium
Other needs: Plastic wrap, a sea sponge, feather

Procedure

Prepare the frame and basecoat with two coats of Moss Green. Sand lightly with a fine paper.

Apply one coat of Jo Sonja's Clear Glazing Medium. While drying, mix equal parts of Green Oxide and Jo Sonja's 'Faux Finish' Kleister Medium. Tear off four pieces of plastic wrap. Apply the mix, and then gently marble with the plastic wrap and remove. When dry, apply one coat of Clear Glazing Medium.

Mix some Carbon Black with Kleister Medium and sponge it very lightly on some areas of the frame. Pounce this area with the large brush. This just spreads the black paint lighter again. Refer to the colour plate frequently for comparison.

Put a little alcohol on a lid and lightly spatter this area, small circles should appear.

When dry, apply one coat of Clear Glazing Medium. Put out a little Smoked Pearl mixed with a little water. With the feather or liner brush, draw some fine lines here and there. When pressure is applied to the liner brush or feather and pulled over to one side, the line will widen into feathery lines, wobbles and twists. Practise this painting on the back of the frame or on paper first. Pounce these lines to soften them.

Spatter some Pale Gold, here and there. The purchased frame had a band of Pale Gold on the inner border which was plastic. I painted this with Pale Gold.

When completely dry, apply the gloss varnish. The more varnish applied the better the finish looks. A very light sanding may be needed between coats.

Well done! Marbling is quite fascinating to do and looks great on many items of furniture, trunks etc. Enjoy.

e more varnish applied the
e needed between coats.

d looks great on many items

75

Small tortoiseshell frame

This frame was purchased in a set of three. When painted, they would look lovely hanging on a velvet band on the wall with three types of cats or other small subjects.

Please note that all materials for the medium and large frames are also listed below.

Techniques

Washes, dragging, varnishing, tortoiseshell

Requirements

Paints: Jo Sonja's Raw Sienna, Raw Umber, Burnt Sienna, Burgundy, Yellow Ochre, Rich Gold and Pale Gold, Carbon Black

Brushes: No. 3 and no. 5 round, a large chinese brush, pouncing

Mediums: Jo Sonja's Clear Glazing Medium, Jo Sonja's 'Faux Finish' Kleister Medium, Rubbing Alcohol

Other needs: Magic Tape, plastic wrap, scissors, ruler, pen

Procedure

Apply two coats of Yellow Ochre to the entire frame. With a

77

no. 3 round brush, make some small daubs with Raw Sienna. Please refer to the colour plate to see the direction of the brush strokes.

Apply some daubs of Raw Umber close to these strokes, and then apply one coat of Jo Sonja's Clear Glazing Medium. Just before the glaze dries, drag some little wisps of the paint down the stroke. Note that the strokes are small because the frame is small. Paint the sides with strokes and washes.

When dry, apply a wash of Burnt Sienna over the finish. The washes dry lighter so it is better to start with a pale wash and, when it is dry, apply another darker one if needed.

Apply several coats of gloss varnish.

Medium tortoiseshell frame

Because we are painting a larger frame, a larger pattern can be painted.

Techniques
Washes, dragging, varnishing, tortoiseshell

Requirements
Please refer to the frame Small tortoiseshell for a list of requirements

Procedure
Basecoat the frame with Yellow Ochre. Apply one coat of Jo Sonja's Clear Glazing Medium

When the medium is dry, use a no. 5 round brush to apply some quick strokes diagonally across the frame with Raw Sienna. Place some dabs and strokes of Raw Umber near the last strokes. Refer to the colour plate for reference.

Put some dabs of Raw Sienna on the Raw Umber, and Raw Umber on the Raw Sienna, just drag diagonally. Apply one coat of Clear Glazing Medium.

Put some rubbing alcohol in a lid and while the Clear Glazing Medium is still wet, pick up some alcohol in the brush and tap it here and there near some of the strokes. Not too many blobs, just enough to soften the paint here and there. With the brush, pull down some diagonal lines with wispy tails. When dry, apply one coat of Clear Glazing Medium

Make a small wash of Burgundy and water and apply it over this surface. Dry. Make a wash of Burnt Sienna, and apply. Stop when you like the effect, or apply another Burgundy wash.

Don't forget to paint the sides of the frame. Gloss varnish.

This effect is well worth all your efforts. Don't be afraid to experiment with colours, I have seen a red and a green tortoiseshell and they look great. It is the washes that make this finish on this frame.

Large tortoiseshell frame

This large frame is really a lesson in inlay; copying tortoiseshell, an exotic wood, ebony and gold. Often pearl shell and stones were included. This is quite an exacting and slow procedure, however using Magic Tape helps make straight lines.

This type of inlay was in vogue during the 17th and 18th centuries and some wonderful examples survive today. I am sure you have seen and perhaps own some beautiful inlay furniture.

The frame needs to have a minimum width of 4 cm ($1^1/_2$"), otherwise the effect is lost. Take time with this project, you might want to do a table or furniture one day, and you want to enjoy the experience. Frames are just the beginning.

Techniques
Washes, dragging, varnishing, tortoiseshell

Requirements
Refer to the 'Small tortoiseshell frame' for a list of requirements.

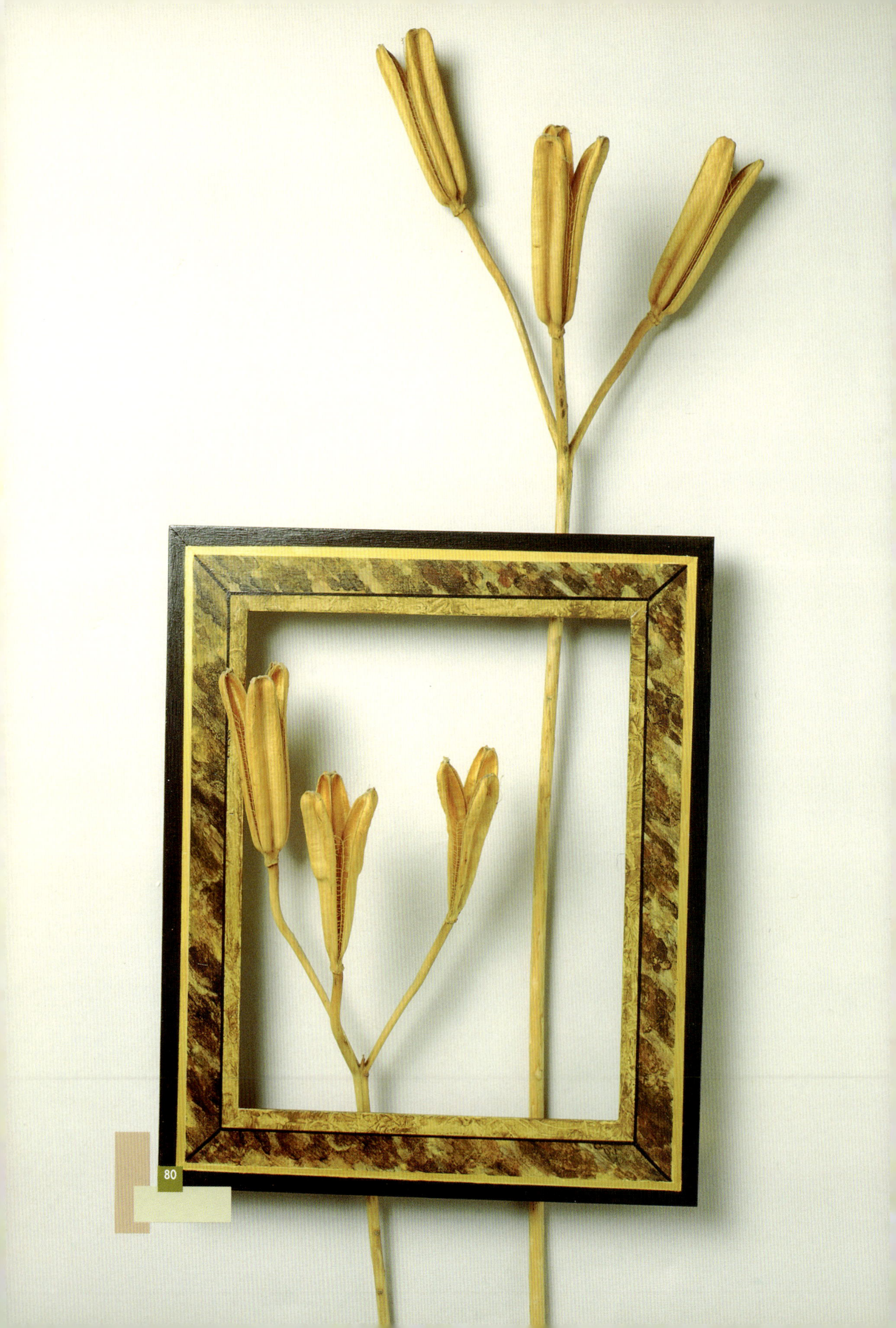

Procedure

Basecoat the frame with two coats of Yellow Ochre. Lightly sand. A very smooth base is needed.

Note when using Magic Tape that only the edges need to be pressed down to prevent bleeding. Do not use a hairdryer to dry the paint while the Magic Tape is on the frame as it might lift the paint.

Apply one coat of Jo Sonja's Clear Glazing Medium and dry. The exotic timber band on the inner frame is 1 cm ($^3/_8$"). And the remaining 2 cm ($^3/_4$") has a small black band and the gold band and the tortoiseshell, so the work is all very accurate. The black lines on the corners were masked off or can be hand painted. The outer black band is 1 cm ($^3/_8$") wide. The sides are also black.

Measure 1 cm ($^3/_8$") for the inner frame and apply Magic Tape. Mix equal parts of Jo Sonja's 'Faux Finish' Kleister Medium, Raw Sienna and Raw Umber, and dab the mix onto the inner frame. Have ready four pieces of plastic wrap. Using one piece for each side, push the plastic around, scrunch it up a little and lift it off gently when you like the effect. Remove the tape. Allow the paint to dry and apply one coat of Clear Glazing Medium over the top. This is the exotic wood effect.

Apply the Magic Tape 1 cm ($^3/_8$") in from the outer frame. Mask off with the tape and apply two nice even coats of Carbon Black. Dry and apply one coat of Clear Glazing Medium

When this is dry, mask off a narrow border for the gold. Keep referring to the colour plate for placement. Use the Rich Gold first, at least two coats, and then dry brush here and there along this line with Pale Gold. Remove the tape and apply Clear Glazing Medium

Now that the inner border is dry, the very fine black ebony border can be painted. One coat of Clear Glazing Medium can be applied. The remaining wide band is now ready for the tortoiseshell finish. These outside borders are masked off to allow for this painting.

Put out a little Clear Glazing Medium and mix in with all the paints we use for the Tortoiseshell.

Dab some strokes with the no. 5 round brush and Raw Sienna diagonally over this area around the frame. Just dab, do not make strokes.

Dab some Red Earth near this. Lightly stroke Raw Umber, here and there, followed by a little Carbon Black, still leaving some small gaps of Yellow Ochre showing through. While the paint is still wet, with the no. 3 round brush, drag some little wisps of paint here and there. Pounce very lightly with the large brush to blend some of these colours, still working diagonally.

While the paint is still wet, put out some alcohol. Tap some blobs of alcohol here and there, with the brush to soften the paint and make patterns.

When dry apply one coat of Clear Glazing Medium and dry. Make a Burgundy Wash and apply over the surface. Wait for the paint to dry and then remove the tape.

Mask off the corners and paint black. Touch up any little 'bleeds'.

When the paint is completely dry, leave the frame to cure for a couple of days, then gloss varnish.

This is really a technique for advanced painters, so if you have never attempted painting before but have completed this frame, it is a great achievement.

Baby girl's frame

This small frame was designed to introduce you to painting butterfly roses with the flat brush. Roses are among the hardest flowers to paint, yet we all want to start with roses. The blending technique does take practice, but the dimensional pearl paint will cover any tiny errors.

This small frame was designed to introduce you to painting butterfly roses with the flat brush. Roses are among the hardest flowers to paint, yet we all want to start with roses. The blending technique does take practice, but the dimensional pearl paint will cover any tiny errors.

The border on the frame needs to be a minimum 4 cm (1 $\frac{1}{2}$") wide.

Techniques

Flat brush blending, liner work, fantasy marbling, dagger brush

Requirements

Paints: Jo Sonja's Titanium White, Napthol Crimson Basecoat, $\frac{1}{4}$" flat brush, 00 liner, $\frac{1}{4}$" dagger

Brushes:

Mediums: Jo Sonja's 'Faux Finish' Kleister Medium, Clear Glazing Medium

Other needs: Paint Stitching Colourpaint's Pearl Ivory

Procedure

Prepare the frame and apply at least four coats of Titanium White. Sand between the coats as a good coverage is needed.

Mix some pink paint by adding a very small amount of Napthol Crimson to about ten parts Titanium White. The colours

Cut out a little pink pain
and plate. The pink pain
butterfly roses go on the w

need to be a good contrast so the marbling effect is seen.

Tear off four pieces of plastic wrap. Put some of the pink paint in a small container, this is for the roses. Mix equal parts of Jo Sonja's 'Faux Finish' Kleister Medium to the rest of the pink paint. Please refer to the colour picture to see where the pink paint will go. It is a wavy line around the frame and on the sides.

Apply one coat of Jo Sonja's Clear Glazing Medium over the white paint, and dry.

Apply the pink mix to the frame. Marble the pink with the plastic wrap. Be careful not to get any of the pink on the white. Use cotton buds to wipe away any mistakes. When dry, apply one coat of Clear Glazing Medium to the whole frame.

Put out a little pink paint and a little Titanium White. Refer to the colour pictures. The pink paint goes on the white side and the white design on the pink side. The butterfly roses go on the white side and the buds on the pink.

The stem goes in a wavy line around the demarcation line. Paint two lines, one pink and one white, going under and over the top of each other like a vine.

With the dagger brush, paint groups of three leaves here and there around the frame. Pink leaves on the white and white leaves on the pink. With the liner brush, paint in some stems and veins, white on pink and pink on white leaves.

Please refer to the technique guidelines for flat brush blending. Practise the technique first and paint the butterfly roses.

When dry, apply two coats of satin varnish.

Squeeze out the Paint Stitching Colourpaint's Pearl Ivory and apply it along the stems. Outline the roses and make some small comma strokes by pulling down some tails from the dots. Apply more dots and generally decorate this painting. Work around the frame to prevent smudging. The pearl paint needs to harden and may take several days. Well done. If it is to be a gift, perhaps you could paint a card to match.

86

Cute teddy frame

See line illustration page 96

Teddy bear cards are numerous and one would look delightful in this frame hanging on a young child's wall. It is not difficult to paint and would look nice hanging on a nursery wall. Don't be too upset when your painting is distressed. You don't have to age your roses and bears, but it is all part of the learning process.

Techniques
Distressing paint, sanding, flat brush blending, dagger brush, liner work, tracing

Requirements
Paints: Jo Sonja's Teal Green Sapphire, Yellow light, Gold Oxide, Napthol Crimson, Green Oxide, Warm White, Carbon Black

Brushes: 1/4" flat blending, fine liner 00, no. 3 round, 1/4" dagger brush

Mediums: Jo Sonja's Clear Glazing Medium

Other needs: Course and fine sandpaper

Procedure
Mix teal green with a little Carbon Black and Clear Glaze Medium. Apply two thick coats. Set aside to dry. Drag paint colours, here and there. Any colours such as blue, cream, white, pale green and red will do. When dry, apply a coat of Velvet Green Basecoat over the whole frame. Some colours can also be applied to the sides of the frame and basecoated.

Fold a small piece of the coarse sandpaper and work over

the green until some of the colours you applied show though. Keep sanding until you have revealed an interesting finish. Do the sides as well. Some of the paler colours can be sanded back to reveal some of the first layer of green paint.

Fold a small piece of fine sandpaper and go over the frame until you have a nice smooth finish. Dust with an old brush or soft cloth and apply one coat of Clear Glazing Medium.

You are now ready to paint the design. Please refer to the black and white design and to the colour print. Trace the design and apply it to the frame. Freehand the design if you can. The roses on my card were blue, but please alter the colours if your card is not the same. There are a series of these cards and the colours differ.

To paint the roses and leaves, please refer to the flat brush blending technique, black and white design and colour plate.

The ribbons are made with the liner brush, a loose mix of Sapphire tipped into Warm White and painted in a wavy line. Make a line with the carbon pencil and when dry remove with the kneadable eraser.

To paint the teddies, put out a little Gold Oxide and Yellow Light. With the no. 3 round brush, paint in some shadows under the neck, feet and ears with Gold Oxide. Lightly dab some Yellow Light on the bears leaving a little shadow. A pouncing or dabbing motion with the tip of the brush makes a fur-like paint finish. When dry, paint a bow on the neck with fine liner brush. Then paint tiny black dots for the eyes and a tiny line for the mouth.

The balloons are painted with your choice of colours. Make a tiny white dot for the highlight on the balloons, then paint the ties and strings.

When completely dry, using a new piece of fine sandpaper, lightly sand over your painting.

Dust off and – when you are happy with the result – apply two coats of satin varnish.

This distressed paint looks lovely painted with other colours. A very old method similar to this one was done with red, black and then lacquered. The black was the basecoat, the red was applied on top, then lightly distress and finished with a very high gloss lacquer. The opposite works well too. The old methods were very time consuming, certain ingredients had to be found and the varnishing done by master craftsmen. Today with our modern paints and knowledge ordinary people, like myself, can attempt some of these finishes.

Red & gold frame

The finish on the frame resembles a course-textured leather. It is an exciting finish, which has many exciting and colour combinations. I chose Christmas colours.

This lovely red and gold textured frame is a new and exciting finish worthy of interesting items to be framed. The technique is about manipulating paint with many colour combinations are possible.

Techniques
Slip slap, dry brushing

Requirements
Paint: Jo Sonja's Burgundy, Napthol Crimson, Napthol Light, Pale Gold

Brushes: Basecoat, no. 10 roymac, shader cs 26

Procedure

Basecoat the entire frame Burgundy.

Put out puddles of the reds on a palette. With the no. 10 brush pick up a large amount of the Napthol Crimson and put it onto several areas on one side of the frame. Pick up some Burgundy paint and repeat the process, slip slap as you go to mix a new colour. At the same time push the paint into the ridges. Pick up the Napthol Light and apply here and there, slip slap, making ridges as you paint. There should be some lovely and different reds showing up.

Move onto the next side and repeat the process. Try not to smudge the work. Do not hasten the drying time with a hair dryer because we want the ridges in the paint to dry thoroughly from the bottom up, so please set them to dry overnight.

Take a good look at the dried finish, you can still work more paint onto this and repeat the process. The higher the ridges, the better the gold will look. Please refer to the colour worksheet and photo.

When thoroughly dried, put out some Pale Gold and a paper towel. With the flat brush, dry brush these ridges with the gold. Keep the brush dry and add more gold where you like.

You should be thrilled with the result, especially when you have applied several coats of gloss or satin varnish.

91

92

Gold leafed mirror

This frame has been gilded with three types of dutch metal: a silver, a gold and an anodized copper. You might like to use only one colour. All the colours come in pads with wax paper between each sheet, and full printed instructions. Art shops are the main suppliers.

This frame has been antiqued, but if you do not like the effect it is not necessary to do it. Painting, colour and finishing are all about choices.

You have to be in the mood to do gold leafing and you need to be organized for success. It is a slow process. Work a small area at a time. Be really organized before you start, and work in a draught free area with no sneezing or heavy breathing!

Gilding is a slow process requiring patience, but once you have the rhythm then there will be no stopping you, nothing will be safe from you. I have gilded mirrors, frames, furniture, boxes, etc. I have painted designs on top of the leaf and I love gilding.

Techniques
Spattering, gold leafing, antiquing

Requirements
Paints: Jo Sonja's Yellow Oxide, Rich Gold and Pale Gold – if painting an object, such as a shell, to glue onto the frame

Brushes: Basecoat, no. 5 round, old toothbrush, a large chinese brush

Mediums: Jo Sonja's Retarder & Antiquing Medium, Rubbing Alcohol, Jo Sonja's Clear Glazing Medium, Jo Sonja's Tannin Sealer and Gold Size

Other needs: Dutch metal, cotton gloves, scissors, cake of soap, cotton balls

Procedure

Remove the backing and mirror from the frame. Set the mirror aside in a safe place. The backing can be painted later if you wish.

Prepare and sand the frame. A nice smooth finish makes a good working surface.

Basecoat the frame with two coats of Yellow Oxide. Sand the frame.

Clean up your work area. Allow plenty of room to move the frame around. A lazy Susan is useful for turning the frame around. Have a hair dryer handy. Keep the leaf in separate containers with lids. Cut the leaf into halves or quarters depending on the size of your frame. Handle leaf carefully, put on cotton gloves and always pick it up with the wax paper facing towards you. Do not get any size on your gloves as it is very sticky and may pick up the leaf and tear. Don't worry if the leaf tears, you can keep the torn pieces in a container and use them for any gaps that may need to be filled. Often small silver pieces look great on gaps in the gold, for instance.

Put out some Jo Sonja's Tannin Sealer and Gold Size and apply it smoothly to a small area about the size of the cut leaf. When almost dry, apply another coat of the sealer. This is the size. Try the sealer again and if it is slightly tacky it is ready to receive the leaf.

Put on your gloves. Pick up a piece of leaf and wax paper and place it gently down on the size. Rub your finger around on the wax. You will feel it adhering. If the size is not applied evenly then ridges will appear in the leaf. If this should happen, then a hair dryer on a warm setting may soften the size and you can smooth out the ridges. However, practice makes perfect. I don't mind a few ridges and tears because, when antiquing the leaf, it looks aged and used. Be careful of the hair dryer and do not use it near the cut gold leaf.

Apply more size, if there are any gaps you can overlap or butt one edge up against the other when changing colours. It is a lot like patchwork. You can always wait for an area to dry then come back again. Apply more size and leaf. Wash brushes frequently.

The sides of the frame are gold leafed too, so use the same colour or use another colour like the anodized one. When you become more experienced, a whole sheet can be applied.

Tip: I keep all the little tailings and when I have saved enough, I paint a black frame, apply size, and with a pair of tweezers glue on all these little tailings.

When all the leaf has been applied, I like to put on some cotton gloves and go round the frame with the hair dryer rubbing over the leaf with my thumb.

Set the frame to dry overnight.

In the morning you will need cotton balls, a cake of soap and some warm water. Put some soap onto a dampened cotton ball and gently wipe it over the leaf.

Any little loose pieces will come off. Repeat the process. Go over any gaps again with size and leaf and then clean up again. Dry.

If you do not wish to antique the frame, apply two coats of satin varnish. If you have found an interesting object to put on your frame, this too can be gold leafed or painted gold. I chose a shell, it was basecoated Rich Gold and dry brushed with Pale Gold, then glued onto the gold leafed frame. Ceramic cherubs look wonderful too.

If antiquing, apply one coat of Clear Glazing Medium. Mix a small amount of the antiquing paints (see directions for antiquing in the section 'Getting Started.') and apply them lightly to the frame. While they are still wet, spatter some alcohol and watch some interesting shapes emerge.

When dry, apply two coats of satin varnish. Replace the mirror and backing.

You have completed a wonderful project. Congratulations and well done!

Congratulations and well done!

Wedding frame

Leather frame

Distressed daisy frame

Cute teddy frame